AN EMBATTLED PRIEST

THE LIFE OF
FATHER OLIVER SHERMAN PRESCOTT
1824-1903

JERVIS S. ZIMMERMAN

authorHOUSE®

AuthorHouse™
1663 Liberty Drive
Bloomington, IN 47403
www.authorhouse.com
Phone: 1-800-839-8640

Published by AuthorHouse   08/28/2012

ISBN: 978-1-4772-5485-1 (sc)
ISBN: 978-1-4772-5483-7 (hc)
ISBN: 978-1-4772-5484-4 (e)

Library of Congress Control Number: 2012913897

Father Oliver Sherman Prescott

CONTENTS

ACKNOWLEDGMENTS

Many persons have graciously assisted the author in the research which made possible this story. Chief among them are the Rev. Dr. Robert G. Carroon, Archivist and Historiographer of the Diocese of Connecticut who has been of constant help throughout the process. Early on Dr. F. Garner Ranney, Archivist and Historiographer of the Diocese of Maryland provided much valued help. At the end of the project Mr. Arthur H. Criddle and the Rev. Dr. Linda C. Smith-Criddle converted a rough draft into clean, readable copy. Three members of the Society of St. John the Evangelist in Cambridge, Mass, have helped greatly—the Rev. William Russell Page, Jr., the Rev. Dr. Eldridge Pendleton and the late Rev. Robert C. Smith. The author gratefully recognizes the kindness of Mr. Richard F. Mitchell, historian, St. Peter's Church, Ellicott City, Maryland and the Rev. Canon Barry E. B. Swain, Rector, St. Clement's Church, Philadelphia. The Rev. Roger White, Rector, St. Andrew's Church, Kent, Conn. kindly examined the Cowley papers in St. Edward's House, Westminster, London through the good offices of the Rev. Alan Grainge, SSJE in charge of that house. The Rev. Mother Superior of the Community of St. John the Baptist in Mendham, New Jersey kindly provided their biography of Fr. Prescott's sister, Emily, known in that Community as Sister Augustine. The Rev.

Canon Michael T. Malone, Ph.D. the author of an excellent article on Prescott's four trials for heresy in Massachusetts is also the author off an unpublished biography of Bishop Levi S. Ives. The author also thanks his daughter, Sarah J. Zimmerman, of Historic New England, the Rev. E. T. Malone, Jr. of Raleigh, No. Carolina, the Rev. Canon D. Lorne Coyle, Rector of Trinity Church, Newport, R. Is. and Mr. Peter J. Knapp, Archivist, Trinity College, Hartford, Conn. for their help. Finally, thanks are extended to Miss Mary Eleanore Murphy Archivist, Diocese of Massachusetts and Mrs. Betty H. Morris of the Church of the Advent, Boston, Massachusetts.

INTRODUCTION

In the Nineteenth Century, the Episcopal Church in the United States experienced an identity crisis. Episcopalians had always thought of their Church as a Protestant church. But in 1833 with the publication in England of the first of the Tracts for the Times, written by several Anglican theologians at Oxford they were reminded that the Episcopal Church is part of the Church Catholic. The Tracts soon crossed the Atlantic and found a small but receptive readership in the American Episcopal Church. The Tracts called for a more pronounced Churchmanship and sought to recover the Catholic, pre-Reformation heritage of the Church of England. The Tracts continued to appear until 1844 when John Henry Newman published the ninetieth and last one—so controversial that the authors dared not publish any more. Not long thereafter, Newman left the Church of England for the Roman Catholic Church to the dismay of many of his friends and colleagues.

In the American Episcopal Church there were a number of clergy who held a high view of the Church and its sacraments. The Right Reverend Samuel Seabury, the first bishop of Connecticut (and of the Anglican communion outside the British Isles) was one such. Another was the Right Reverend John Henry Hobart, Bishop of New York from 1816 to 1830. Their friends and followers at first warmly welcomed the

Tracts as they began to circulate and be discussed in the United States. But these American Episcopalians were austere and simple in their conduct of worship. Except for the use of the <u>Book of Common Prayer</u> and the presence of bishops, the services of the Episcopal Church at that time looked very much like those of their Protestant neighbors.

But in America, as in England, the younger readers of the Tracts were eager to recover some of the liturgical expressions of the Catholic faith. Many of the men were to be found at the General Theological Seminary of the Episcopal Church in New York City. The changes brought by early ritualists created intense controversy in the Episcopal Church (and in the Church of England) for decades to come. They taught that the Episcopal Church was not just another Protestant denomination, but a part of the undivided Catholic Church, together with the Roman Catholic Church and the Orthodox Churches of the East. And their liturgical innovations began to demonstrate this conviction. Some of these early Tractarian clergy quickly gave up the struggle to work within the Episcopal Church and became Roman Catholics. Those who remained loyal to the Episcopal Church found a small but devoted following of laity in the established Eastern dioceses. Others moved to the "western frontier" then located in Illinois and Wisconsin where newly established dioceses gave them freedom to introduce Catholic liturgical practices and make them the norm in parishes. But wherever they ministered, these early ritualist clergy were an embattled minority.

One such priest was the Reverend Oliver Sherman Prescott. Because of his Tractarian views, particularly his teaching about confession and priestly absolution, he was tried for heresy four times by the Episcopal Bishop of Massachusetts. Prescott was also one of the first priests in the Episcopal Church with a clear and continuing vocation to the monastic life. In 1847—the very month of his ordination as a deacon— Prescott became a part of the short-lived Society of the Holy Cross under Bishop Levi S. Ives of North Carolina. In 1868 Prescott became one of the first members of the Society of St. John the Evangelist at Cowley, near Oxford, England—the earliest continuing monastic community for men to be established in England since the Reformation. In 1879, Prescott was tried and admonished by the Bishop of Pennsylvania for his ritual practices at St. Clement's Church in Philadelphia of which Prescott was Rector. Despite these and other vicissitudes, Prescott remained loyal to the Episcopal Church all his life. This is the story of his life and priestly labors. Thanks to the extent of his correspondence which has survived, it can be told largely in Prescott's own words.

CONNECTICUT: EARLY YEARS

Oliver Prescott was born in New Haven, Connecticut on March 25, 1824 into a large and prosperous family. His grandfather, Benjamin Prescott, became in 1794 a business partner of Roger Sherman, Jr., the son of the signer of the Declaration of Independence. The younger Sherman was also Benjamin Prescott's brother-in-law, having married Prescott's sister. Prescott and Sherman kept a store in New Haven across Chapel Street from Yale College. Here they offered for sale not only food stuff, but also coal, tobacco, cotton, rum, gin and brandy.[1] Their business prospered. When Benjamin Prescott died in 1839 at the age of 82, he left an estate valued at more than $25,000—a substantial sum at the time. The inventory of his household furnishings included his "pleasure carriage" valued at $150.[2] Grandfather Prescott's long business partnership with the younger Roger Sherman explains Oliver's middle name, Sherman.

Oliver's parents were Major Enos Alling Prescott and Mary Carrington. Oliver was the ninth of fourteen children born to them, six of whom died in infancy. Thus, Oliver was one of eight siblings who lived to adulthood. Oliver had three older brothers, Benjamin, Harry, and Enos, Jr., who all eventually entered their father's business. A sister, Mary Rebecca, was born next before Oliver. And another sister,

Emily Augusta, was born immediately after him. These three formed a "triad" and Oliver was close to his two sisters. He also had two younger brothers, William and Frank. There was a span of twenty-six years between the oldest and youngest Prescott child.[3]

Oliver was born and grew up in the Prescott "Long House." This was a remarkable building consisting of three houses attached to each other, each with two full stories and a gambrel roof above. The 18th Century Long House was purchased by Grandfather Benjamin Prescott. He lived in the central portion, Oliver's parents lived in one side and his aunt and uncle, Elizabeth and Henry Hotchkiss, lived in the other side of the Long House.[4]

Because his business was based on the shipping trade, Grandfather Prescott found the Long House on the New Haven harbor convenient. The harbor formed the south boundary of his house lot. Nearby was the Long Wharf in the harbor. Oliver's father was also engaged in the shipping business, dealing in coal and lumber. He was wharfinger, or manager of the Long Wharf, the center of New Haven's shipping trade. Enos A. Prescott was, at various times, a New Haven city alderman, an associate Judge of the City Court, and Vice President of the New Haven Chamber of Commerce. His firm of Prescott & Co. were agents and proprietors of the Boston Line of Packets.[5] From 1823 to 1852 he served as a Vestryman of Trinity Church, New Haven. Through the spouses of Oliver's aunts and uncles, he was related to several prominent New Haven families. Probably sometime after the death of his grandfather, Oliver's parents moved a little further inland from the harbor to 13 Whiting Street, where the family lived for the rest of his parents' lives. This house, like the Long House and, indeed, Whiting Street itself, has long since disappeared.

Because he was sick, Oliver was baptized at home by the Reverend Harry Croswell, Rector of Trinity Church.[6] Croswell read the Tracts for the Times as they reached this country from England and was probably the first priest in Connecticut to advocate their principles. Occasionally in his diary Croswell mentions meeting with parishioners to discuss these Tracts. Croswell's son, William, was the first rector of the Church of the Advent in Boston, a parish organized in 1844 on Tractarian principles. The senior Croswell undoubtedly had a strong influence on Oliver Prescott's spiritual development and future churchmanship.

We do not know where Oliver prepared for college. But, in 1840 he entered Trinity College in Hartford, then called Washington College. He studied here for two years[7] and then, in 1842, entered Yale College. He attended Yale for one year, living in his parents' home on Whiting Street.[8] There is an anecdote in an unsigned manuscript biography of Prescott in the SSJE archives in Cambridge, Massachusetts. It reports that young Prescott was a member of the Brothers in Unity Society at Yale, which met regularly to debate issues. The subject of the debate was King Charles I of England. In the debate, Prescott attacked the judges who condemned King Charles to death as no better than murderers. It was an inflammatory remark indicative of Prescott's high church views. In New Haven the descendants of the Puritans remembered the execution of Charles I as liberation, not murder. This created such a scandal at Yale that Professors Kingsley and Gibbs visited Prescott to discuss his views. The records of the Brothers in Unity Society at Yale record that Prescott was a member in 1842-43.[9] Although some of the topics of their debates are recorded, none mentions King Charles I. If the anecdote is true, it not only reveals Oliver's high church sympathy for Charles I, but also his readiness to boldly express his views come what may. At the end of that academic year, Prescott withdrew from Yale.

On the afternoon of May 28, 1843, Oliver and one of his sisters were confirmed at Trinity Church, New Haven, by Bishop Brownell. In his diary, the Reverend Harry Croswell reports that there were 114 persons in the class, 111 of whom were confirmed.

> "Such a crowd has never appeared there (in Trinity Church) before—aisles, galleries and even the chancel steps were filled. The confirmation was remarkably impressive the number being so large and among them so many heads of families. The proportion of those from the surrounding sects, congregation, Methodist and Baptist, was at about one to five."[10] Croswell preached at the service

We do not know what Oliver did in 1843-44. He probably lived at home and worked with his father and older brothers in the family shipping business. Although he had not graduated from either Trinity College or Yale, and did not have an undergraduate degree, in the fall of 1844 Prescott entered the General Theological Seminary.

On August 5, 1844 Harry Croswell wrote a letter of introduction to the faculty of the General Seminary for Oliver Prescott.[11] Croswell's prominence as a priest would certainly give weight to his recommendation of Prescott. The following year on November 28, 1845, Croswell received a letter from Professor Ogilbie complaining of O.S. Prescott and wishing Croswell to interpose with his friends.[12] The Reverend John David Ogilbie was Professor of Ecclesiastical History at the General Seminary from 1840 to 1851. We don't know the nature of his complaints about Prescott. Although Prescott's ability was apparent, his views made him a maverick in the eyes of more conventional clergy.

Croswell's diary yields one further glimpse of Prescott's distinctive churchmanship. In July 1847, two months before Prescott was ordained deacon, Croswell had to put to rest "some mischievous stories about Prescott and his sister's preparations for trimming the altar."[13] Again, Croswell did not specify of what these altar "trimmings" consisted. Croswell is what might be described as a "high and dry" churchman. He held and taught a high doctrine of the Church in the traditions of Bishop Seabury and Bishop Hobart. But he was "dry," that is, simple and austere in his conduct of worship. At that time even bouquets of garden flowers were forbidden in church, not to mention candles and colored hangings of any sort.

During his examination of Prescott prior to ordination to the deaconate, Bishop Brownell said, "I heard that you are accustomed to make the sign of the cross." To which Prescott replied, "Yes, but not obtrusively. I do not think it would be remarked unless someone was watching. It was made on me at my baptism." The Bishop continued, "I must ask you to discontinue this practice. I will not ordain you unless you promise." To this Prescott replied, "I cannot promise."[14] The other candidate for ordination remonstrated with Prescott to no avail. In any event, the Bishop relented because Prescott was ordained deacon on Thursday, September 16, 1847 in Trinity Church, New Haven. Croswell's son, William, preached. There is in the General Seminary Prescott archives a letter to Oliver from William Croswell dated August 13, 1847 in which Croswell expresses the hope that the date of the ordination may be deferred, if possible, until after the middle of September.[15] For William Croswell to be the preacher at his ordination was evidently something which Prescott very much wanted. The following Sunday, after his ordination, Prescott assisted in the communion for the first time in his home parish.

NORTH CAROLINA: THE SOCIETY OF THE HOLY CROSS

From October 6 to October 28, 1847 the General Convention of the Episcopal Church met in New York City. Bishop Benjamin T. Onderdonk, the Bishop of New York and a leader of the Tractarian party, had been suspended on doubtful charges. His role as leader of the Catholic minded clergy fell to the Right Reverend Levi S. Ives of North Carolina.[16] Ives used his visit to New York City to recruit members for a Society (or Order) of the Holy Cross which he intended to establish. At the same time, Bishop Ives recruited clergy to serve in mission churches in his diocese. Prescott responded to both calls. It is not known exactly when he became a member of the Society of the Holy Cross. Probably he took his vows in Bishop Ives' presence after the Bishop arrived in New York City.

Among the others who joined the Society was another clergyman of the Diocese of Connecticut, the Reverend William Glenney French.[17] He had graduated from the General Theological Seminary in 1842 and wanted to join his classmates who went to Wisconsin to establish Nashotah House. But French's parents were aged and in poor health and he did not feel he could leave them. By 1847 French, now in priest's orders, had experience as a teacher and parish minister and was interested in joining the Society of the Holy Cross. Bishop Ives, as General of the Society, received French into membership in the Society and immediately named him Superior of the community which was to be settled at Valle Crucis in western North Carolina. Sometime in the first week of November 1847 Bishop Ives heard French's vows in St. Luke's Church, New York City, using a simplified version of the form used in the reception of Sisters by the Bishop of New York. The group at Valle Crucis was to consist of French, his younger brother Louis, the Reverend W. R. Gries, a deacon of the Diocese of North Carolina, and Hezekiah Thomas, a protégé of Oliver Prescott. Prescott, although a member of the Order (or Society), was to be in charge of a mission church at Mocksville, North Carolina many miles east of Valle Crucis.

The day after he professed his vows, French was taken by Prescott on a shopping expedition to a Roman Catholic Church supplies store where they bought a crucifix, several French devotional pictures, an Ursuline manual of prayer (which French adapted for use with the boys in the Valle Crucis school), and letter paper headed with a picture of St. Francis Xavier. They also visited the Roman Catholic Cathedral on Prince Street to study ecclesiastical robes, altar cloths, and clergy vestments. French notes that:

> "Prescott was at that time intimate with some Roman Catholic priests in the city who were evidently cajoling him, with the expectation of accomplishing his conversion; though I have often thought that as far as the outward show, the aesthetics of their Church was concerned, there needed to be no effort made, for there was nothing of that sort that seemed to him to be objectionable."[18]

On November 5, 1847, French and Prescott, along with young Louis French and Hezekiah Thomas, left New York City. En route they

7

stopped briefly in Baltimore and visited the Roman Catholic Cathedral there. They were favorably impressed with the fact that it was open and in use by devout persons while all of the Episcopal Churches they tried to enter were closed on that week-day. Eventually, they reached Raleigh, North Carolina, where the Reverend Mr. Gries joined them. This marked the end of their journey by public transportation and the beginning of a two week trek. They rented a wagon for their goods and Bishop Ives loaned them a team of large horses. On November 15 the party of five left Raleigh with two Negroes, one of whom served as driver and guide, and the other as cook for the journey as well as the school when they reached Valle Crucis. The five young men (and presumably the cook, as well) all journeyed on foot. After four days traveling about 75 miles on foot, they reached Greensboro where Prescott left them to go to Mocksville nearby. He and French never saw each other again in North Carolina.

Our concern here is not with the brief life of the Order at Valle Crucis.[19] Nor is it with Bishop Ives' resignation and eventual conversion to the Roman Catholic Church.[20] Prescott walked from Greensboro to Mocksville where he began his ministry at tiny St. Phillip's Church and in adjacent communities. St. Phillip's consisted of two families and nine communicants. St. Andrew's Church, in Rowan County, listed 47 communicants. And Christ Church, also in Rowan County, listed 87 communicants. Prescott, in deacon's orders that first year, could not celebrate the Eucharist. But he had baptisms in each congregation. And he undertook his parochial duties with the energy and enthusiasm which was to characterize his subsequent parochial cures.

Prescott, in his youthful enthusiasm, wanted to shout from the housetops the word about the Society of the Holy Cross and its vows. Bishop Ives counseled discretion, indeed, silence.

A great fuss is made about vows of celibacy. Now what I
ask is, that you shall say nothing about yours and those of
others. It is a matter of right which no one has any business
to interfere with—and hence to know about. Our wisdom is
to keep silence. The most innocent expressions are tortured
into revelations of popish plots, etc.[21]

In keeping with his Tractarian principles, Prescott reported to
the Diocese that in St. Philip's Church "the Holy Days have been
observed and during Lent daily prayers were said." There were very
few city Episcopal churches where that happened, let alone tiny rural
congregations. On March 9, 1848, Harry Croswell wrote Prescott
commending him for introducing frequent services. Croswell writes:

Nothing will go so far to convince the people among
whom you are laboring of the importance of prayer and the
reading of the Scriptures, the distinguishing characteristics
of the Catholic and Apostolic Church. And for yourself, as
you seem to be well aware, the exercise will (. . .) be most
salutary.[22]

Croswell further urges Prescott to be ordained priest as soon
as possible and hints at opportunities which might await him in the
North.

By July 26, 1848, Prescott was in New Haven where Bishop
Brownell wrote him giving his permission for Bishop Ives to ordain
Prescott to the priesthood in Trinity Church, New Haven.[23] Before
the ordination could take place, Prescott had to be examined by the
Connecticut Diocesan Standing Committee. Harry Croswell reports in

his Diary on August 12 that at that examination, the Reverend Thomas C. Pitkin, Croswell's assistant in Trinity Church, was "very cautious in his examination of Prescott."[24] Prescott's reputation as a "high churchman" had clearly reached the Connecticut Standing Committee. The ordination took place the next day, Sunday, at Trinity Church, New Haven, with Bishop Ives officiating and preaching the sermon. Croswell describes the service in his Diary:

> "The ordination had been anticipated with much interest and some anxiety, the latter (Prescott) especially having been the object of great prejudice and not a little persecution."[25]

Croswell's remarks clearly foreshadowed what was in store for Prescott.

On October 12, 1848, Bishop Ives visited Mocksville and consecrated St. Philip's Church, apparently constructed under Prescott's tenure there.[26] In his Diocesan address the following May, Bishop Ives reported that Prescott had removed from St. Philip's Church, having been kept from stated service there during the winter owing to ill health. By October 1849, Prescott had begun assisting the Rector of the Church of the Advent in Boston, the Reverend William Croswell, son of his family's priest. And on November 14, 1849, Prescott's canonical residence was transferred from North Carolina to Massachusetts.[27]

BOSTON: THE FOUR TRIALS FOR HERESY

The Church of the Advent in Boston had been founded in 1844 as a Tractarian parish and the Reverend Dr. William Croswell was its first rector. For some time the Bishop of Massachusetts, the Right Reverend Manton Eastburn, had taken strenuous exception to certain liturgical practices at the Church of the Advent—the presence of a simple cross behind the altar, the refusal of the clergy to celebrate the Holy Communion from the "north end" of the altar, and the fact that the clergy wore surplices instead of black gowns. As a consequence, Bishop Eastburn refused to visit the parish for confirmation. And, at that time, there was no national canon in the Episcopal Church requiring the bishop to visit each congregation at least once in every three years. Prescott, in his move to Boston, was back in New England close to his family home. He was working in a parish and with a priest sympathetic to his Tractarian churchmanship. But he was entering a Diocese whose bishop was hostile to those principles.

Prescott's tenure as assistant at the Church of the Advent was brief. By June 1850, he had resigned.[28] Shortly thereafter he met with Bishop Eastburn to discuss other clerical employment in the Diocese of Massachusetts. In the course of this meeting, Prescott freely expressed his theological views. The Bishop was horrified at what he heard and promptly shared it with the Standing Committee of the Diocese who drew up a presentment against Prescott.[29] On July 17, 1850, Prescott was served with this presentment which outlined six charges and 32 specifications against him. The charges included teaching that the Virgin Mary was a sinless "object of worship," encouraging the use of the "Hail Mary," teaching transubstantiation and teaching that private auricular confession was allowable and that the priestly absolution

11

thereafter was valid and permissible. In the conduct of worship, he was charged with turning his back on the congregation at certain times in the service.

Prescott was fortunate in securing as his attorney, Richard Henry Dana, Jr., who was a vestryman of the Church of the Advent. He had published Two Years Before the Mast, in 1840. The first trial began on November 26, 1850 and lasted only three days. Dana attacked the presentment and pointed out so many flaws in it that the court, consisting of five clergy of the Diocese, agreed that it was faulty and null and void. Dana also attacked the manner in which the court had been constituted, finding it flawed, with which the court did not agree. In any event, the charges were quashed and the first trial ended in a victory for Prescott and Dana.

However, the Bishop was not about to give up the struggle easily. On March 3, 1851, the Standing Committee drew up a new presentment against Prescott and forwarded it to the Bishop to sign. Prescott had now been unemployed for more than six months and financially dependent on his father. On February 10, 1851, the Reverend Harry Croswell wrote to President Millard Fillmore in favor of the appointment of Oliver Prescott to a chaplaincy in the U.S. Navy.[30] On the same day, Oliver's father wrote to U.S. Senator Roger S. Baldwin requesting his support for Oliver's application for a navy chaplaincy.[31] In view of the Prescott family's long maritime connections, this proposal may have come from Oliver's father.

Senator Baldwin duly wrote the Secretary of the Navy on Oliver's behalf. But nothing came of it. It is hard to imagine that a Navy chaplaincy would have afforded much scope for Oliver's churchmanship.

When the Navy Chaplaincy fell through, Prescott began ministering at St. Botolph's Church in Boston in Lent, 1851. This apparently was a group of Catholic minded Episcopalians who, encouraged by William Croswell, had rented a hall on Washington Street. The congregation was never formally recognized by the Diocese and the Bishop chastised Prescott for serving there. Bishop Eastburn personally delivered the second presentment to Prescott at his home at #1 Staniford Street in Boston, and ordered Prescott to stop ministering at St. Botolph's.

On April 14, 1851, Prescott wrote his old friend, William G. French, in Milford, Connecticut, urging him to join him at St. Botolph's Church which he had begun to serve two weeks earlier. Prescott wrote:

> The Bishop pounced upon me without so much as asking my leave, or begging my pardon: served on me a second presentment, and without assigning any reason required me to desist from officiating at St. Botolph's, a requisition which I very respectfully declined yielding to, so long as he refused to give the grounds on which he bases his authority to make it.

Prescott then urges French to "run a little risk of Episcopal disapproval and accept the appointment" to serve with him in a collegiate ministry at St. Botolph's. He concludes "a few months will decide for us personally whether Massachusetts will have the Catholic system . . ."[32]

As with his first trial, so with the second one, Prescott objected to the clergy proposed by the Bishop to serve on the trial court. Prescott found them to be young, inexperienced, often dependent on the Bishop for their living, and of an Evangelical persuasion. On June 28, 1851, Prescott published his correspondence with Bishop Eastburn, thereby increasing the tensions between the Bishop and himself. The controversy was attracting considerable attention in the secular and church press. Both sides hoped the trial would establish a clear victory for their party and its theology.

The second trial began on July 1, 1851 and Richard Henry Dana, Jr. again represented Prescott. Dana contended that because the court was a court of special and limited jurisdiction, it was essential that every fact pertaining to its creation and jurisdiction should be clearly established. None of the five diocesan priests who constituted the court were learned in the law and Dana's careful questioning into the way in which summonses had been served and other details struck the court as unnecessary delaying tactics. The court was eager to get on with the consideration of the five charges against Prescott. At the beginning of the second day of the trial Dana called for the record of the first day's proceedings and was told that none had been kept. Dana then wrote a protest both on the evidence of the court's authority and its failure to keep a record of its proceedings which the court refused to enter into the record. Finally, on July 3, the third day of the trial, Dana and Prescott withdrew from the court which promptly recommended that Prescott be suspended from the exercise of the ministry until such time as he should reappear to answer the charges and, if he had not done so within six months, he was to be deposed from the ministry.[33]

Two days later, Eastburn pronounced the sentence of suspension, despite Prescott's written protest to him. The situation was at a stalemate. Prescott would either have to stand trial within six months or be summarily deposed from the ministry. Prescott's plight became widely known in the Episcopal Church. Among those who wrote him offering support was Bishop William Whittingham of Maryland. On November 15, 1851, Prescott wrote Bishop Whittingham thanking him for his expression of sympathy. Prescott wrote Whittingham that he and the Bishop of New Hampshire were the only bishops with whom he was personally unacquainted who had manifested any interest in his troubles.[34] Thus began a relationship that was to continue for many years. Bishop Whittingham had taught church history at the General Theological Seminary before he became Bishop of Maryland. He was sympathetic to the Tractarian's viewpoint.

Prescott, in the same letter, informed Bishop Whittingham that he had demanded a new trial. He also assured the Bishop that he had been, and was, loyal to the Episcopal Church. Prescott concluded

> "the cause of sound churchmanship is humanly speaking so bound up with my being able to prove myself to have been loyal and consistent, that I cannot, for a moment, think of relinquishing at present my position. I ought not, and do not, dread a fair trial."

At the same time Dana wrote Bishop Whittingham[35] responding to his earlier letter supportive of Prescott. Dana expressed the hope that the new trial court will be more fairly constituted. That fall, Dana toyed with the thought of appealing to lay courts which Prescott was not willing to do unless it was "pretty clear that the Church authorities can afford him no relief."[36]

On November 9, 1851, Prescott suffered a personal loss in the sudden death of the Reverend William Croswell, his friend and rector at the Church of the Advent. About that time, Prescott wrote to Bishop Ives requesting release from the vows he had made in the Society of the Holy Cross. On January 16, 1852, Bishop Ives wrote Prescott informing him that the vows ceased to exist when the order was dissolved in the

Spring of 1849.[37] Ives was himself going through the ordeal of leaving the Episcopal Church. In December 1852, Bishop Ives and his wife were received into the Roman Catholic Church in the city of Rome.

The third trial began on February 9, 1852. Again, Prescott had great difficulty in accepting the clergy proposed by the Bishop to serve on the court. Of the nine proposed by Bishop Eastburn, four had served on the preceding court and could not be considered unbiased. Three of the others had been twice rejected by Prescott. Prescott wrote, "I despair of the proceedings against me, and shall submit to it, simply recording my protest, for the benefit of any who may come after me."[38] Two of the members of the court in the second trial also sat on the court in the third trial.

The first charge pertained to Prescott's statement in a sermon that the Virgin Mary was the "sinless parent of a sinless child." Prescott had decided before the first trial not to use this expression again since it was open to misinterpretation. In any event, Dana pointed out, the subject of this statement was the incarnation and not the Virgin Mary.

The second charge of heresy was that Prescott had taught that auricular confession to a priest is allowable and profitable. Dana cited in rebuttal a long list of noted Anglican theologians in support of private confession to a priest. The court agreed that the first two charges against Prescott were not sustained.

The third heresy charge was that Prescott had taught that "priestly absolution, in connection with and upon auricular confession, is profitable and desirable to individuals and allowed by the Church."[39] Here Dana cited the sentence in the service of ordination of a priest, "whose sins thou dost forgive, they are forgiven and whose sins thou dost retain, they are retained." Dana then asked, "Does she give her clergy a power and punish them for teaching that they have it?"[40] He then went on to cite a long list of Anglican authorities back to and including Archbishop Cranmer on the authority of priestly absolution, both in private and public pronouncements.

The fourth charge was that Prescott had violated the Constitution of the Episcopal Church by declaring that the Thirty-Nine Articles were "worthless and of no binding obligation on him."[41] The fifth charge was of "immoral conduct" for making the same statement.[42] These two charges were essentially the same and neither of them was sustained at the trial.

It was only of the third charge that Prescott was found guilty. And here the court found him guilty, not of heresy, but of an "irregularity." In his closing address to the court, Dana spoke for six hours and said that "nearly every man in the room shed tears."[43] But to no avail. The court recommended that Bishop Eastburn require Prescott to sign a statement indicating his willingness to refrain from teaching the value and effectiveness of priestly absolution pronounced privately to a penitent, and to be suspended from functioning as a priest until he signed such a statement.

Bishop Eastburn pronounced the sentence on March 15, 1852 in Prescott's absence. Dana had appealed to the Bishop to postpone the announcement until Prescott had returned to Boston, but to no avail. If the second trial ended in a stalemate, the third trial confronted Prescott with a painful dilemma. To sign the statement meant denying his most deeply held convictions about the priesthood. But not signing the statement meant that he could not exercise the priesthood. Nor could he be transferred to another diocese as long as he was under sentence of suspension in Massachusetts. On May 5, 1852, Prescott wrote Bishop Whittingham seeking his advice and counsel.[44] Prescott was considering appealing Eastburn's decision to the civil courts, but would not do so before pursuing channels for redress in his Church.

Meanwhile, strange as it may seem, Bishop Eastburn and the Standing Committee were preparing for a fourth trial of Prescott! This time he was charged with violating the sentence of suspension of July 1851 which had automatically lapsed when Prescott applied for a new trial (his third). Prescott readily admitted that he had done this, on competent legal advice, believing the first sentence was illegal and the court itself invalid. The fourth trial took place May 21, 1852. Prescott was duly found guilty and the sentence was "paternal admonition." Dana wrote in his Diary:

> When the Bishop tried to convict him (Prescott) of heresy, he selected the lowest Churchmen he could find. When the charge was contumacy, and the point was the extent of the Bishop's authority, he selected a court of high-churchmen.[45]

Of the sentence itself, Dana wrote: "It was a solemn farce, enlivened by the bitterness of the Bishop, who gave his censure greater force by professions of friendliness."[46] Of the Bishop himself, Dana wrote: "The B. is a shallow man. A man of little brain, little heart, but conceited, self-willed and self-indulgent. No reliance can be placed on his honor or generosity."[47]

In January 1852, Prescott again wrote Bishop Whittingham. Prescott's deep personal anguish is painfully evident in this letter. He says that Dana, who is still serving as his counsel, was considering a petition to the Supreme Court on a writ of mandamus to require Bishop Eastburn to restore Prescott. Dana eventually decided against this action. Prescott, meanwhile proposed to Bishop Eastburn an alternate document regarding priestly absolutions in which he promised

"While under the actual and canonical jurisdiction of the Right Reverend Manton Eastburn, D.D., to refrain from teaching and inculcating that a Presbyter of the Church in this Diocese, etc."[48]

Bishop Eastburn refused to accept this compromise statement.

Prescott had also written to the Reverend Edward B. Pusey, in Oxford, England, for his counsel. Pusey's reply is dated November 12, 1852.[49] He responded favorably to the modified certificate which Prescott was willing to sign (apparently not yet knowing that Bishop Eastburn had refused its wording.) on condition that letters dimissory immediately be granted to the Diocese of Maryland. This indicates that as early as this date, Bishop Whittingham was considering accepting Prescott in the Diocese of Maryland. Prescott must have forwarded Dr. Pusey's letter to Bishop Whittingham, which would explain how it ended up in the Maryland Diocesan Archives. Dr. Pusey further pointed out that a priest prohibited by his Diocesan cannot absolve. But he says neither does a priest have the right to acquiesce to permanently not exercising that function. This still left Prescott hung on the horns of a dilemma. Pusey said that he himself would not like to employ a civil court to control a bishop. "It is utterly wrong in principle."[50] Finally, Pusey thinks that the Bishop must have used "a living" in a technical sense, and that he would have secured to Prescott food and raiment. Dr. Pusey overestimated Bishop Eastburn's generosity!

Having decided against appealing Bishop Eastburn's decision to the civil courts, the only channel open to Prescott was to appeal to the General Convention of the Church when it met in New York City in October 1853: There was historic precedent for such an appeal. In 1808, the Reverend Ammi Rogers, a priest of the Diocese of Connecticut, had appealed a disciplinary decision of the Bishop of Connecticut to the General Convention and it had been willing to consider his appeal. Prescott was not so fortunate. On October 12, the Lower House (of Clerical and Lay Deputies) refused to allow his memorial to be read by a vote of 57 to 54. On that date, Prescott wrote Bishop Whittingham expressing the hope that he might meet with more success from the House of Bishops.[51] Five days later, Prescott forwarded his petition to Bishop Whittingham.[52] The House of Bishops, after some debate, agreed to have the Memorial read. They found it "respectful," but took no action other than to vote to allow Prescott to withdraw it.

There was nothing else for Prescott to do except to sign the hated document, which he did on October 22. On November 2, 1853, Bishop Eastburn transferred Prescott to the Diocese of Maryland and Prescott's long ordeal was at an end.[53] However, he continued to have painful misgivings about having signed the agreement, even though it was the only way he could salvage his ministry. Bishop Whittingham wrote Prescott on December 16, 1853 that he considered

> "said sentence and certificate as irregular, unlawful and of no force or account beyond the diocese in which the said court had jurisdiction."[54]

Bishop Whittingham is quoted as having said, "What a Bishop could do a Bishop could undo."[55]

MARYLAND: ASCENSION CHURCH, WESTMINSTER

In October 1853, Bishop Whittingham had received an appeal for help in finding a priest to serve Ascension Church in Westminster, Maryland.[56] The letter was written by Miss Lucretia Van Bibber, daughter of a prominent Baltimore family who also maintained a summer home called "Avondale" two miles from Westminster. Miss Van Bibber expressed the hope that while the Bishop was in New York attending the General Convention of the Church, he might encounter "some missionary spirit willing to undertake so self-denying a charge." Miss Van Bibber continued,

> "the parish is unable to take care of itself; the formality of a
> Vestry meeting is no longer attempted . . . It seems to depend
> upon us and we continue to identify ourselves with it and to
> love it."

Miss Van Bibber and her widowed mother were both Catholic-minded ladies whose husband (and father) had built the beautiful little church and was buried in its churchyard. This was the parish that the Bishop offered to Prescott. The Bishop made it clear that there was only a handful of people in the parish and that the post was truly a missionary one.[57] Prescott was eager to begin ministering at Westminster after his three year suspension from priestly functioning. He hoped to begin Advent with a special evening service.[58] But in reply, the Bishop counseled that

"it will be some time, I fear, before you can ripen matters far
enough to be able to rejoice in extra services such as that you
purpose, by way of introduction to Advent."[59]

On August 15, 1854, Prescott wrote the Bishop enclosing
testimonials for Charles C. Grafton required for his admittance as a
candidate for Holy Orders in the Diocese of Maryland.[60] Grafton met
Prescott in 1849 when he was assistant to the Rector at the Church of
the Advent. Grafton was then nineteen years old, six years Prescott's
junior. Grafton remembered asking Prescott in the early fifties whether
he supposed there were any other Tractarians than the two of them
in America.[61] Grafton was confirmed in May 1851 in Dr. William
Croswell's last confirmation class before his death. In 1851, Grafton
entered Harvard Law School, having prepared by study at the Boston
Latin School and, briefly, at Phillips Andover Academy. During this
time, he and Prescott continued seeing each other. Prescott had moved
to Cambridge in 1852. Grafton said:

"The Reverend Father Prescott told me that if God intended
me to be a third-rate clergyman, rather than a first-class lawyer,
my duty was to enter the ministry rather than to seek the other
profession. One must seek first to know one's vocation, and
then trust God and follow it. It was thus, partly under his
influence, that I had the courage to offer myself to Bishop
Whittingham of Maryland, as a candidate for Holy Orders."[62]

Grafton studied privately under Prescott's direction in Westminster,
and was ordained a Deacon by Bishop Whittingham on December 23,
1855. While he was studying in Westminster, Grafton assisted Prescott

in his ministry there. After ordination to the deaconate, Grafton was assigned by the Bishop to the parish in Reisterstown to assist the Reverend Dr. Rich.

Seventeen letters to Bishop Whittingham from Prescott during the three years he served Ascension parish are preserved in the Maryland Diocesan Archives. Their tone is filial, warm and confiding. To Prescott Whittingham was much more than an ecclesiastical administrator. He was Prescott's spiritual pastor and mentor. The letters also give a picture of Prescott at this time of life. He is promptly preparing a class of candidates for confirmation. He has gathered a small congregation nearby at Uniontown. Miss Van Bibber has offered an altar cross for Ascension Church and the Bishop has advised against it. The Bishop was no ritualist. Prescott's disappointment is great; he proposes a plan to gradually introduce the cross into the church; but he dutifully accepts the Bishop's counsel. He asks to be excused from attending the Diocesan Convention because Baltimore "is quite alive with rumors affecting my honor as a gentleman, if not my good name."[63] Prescott almost wishes he could find a position in a foreign church where he could be cut off from the past and begin anew and be judged by what he is and not by that which prejudice and misrepresentation and idle or malicious rumors have made him.[64] He declines an invitation to preach in Pittsfield, Massachusetts and be considered as rector there. If an epidemic of fever breaks out in Baltimore, he offers to come and minister there. If he is to remain in Maryland against his father's wishes, he must be entirely independent of him and this he cannot be on the salary he can depend upon.[65] (His annual salary from the Diocesan Pastoral Aid Fund was $300, plus modest occasional gifts from the parish.) He requests an advance of $175 from the Pastoral Aid Fund in order to repay a loan that is due. He bristles at being informed by the Missionary Committee of the Diocese that he is in <u>their</u> employ. Nor will he agree to collect offerings every Sunday and credit the amount to the Missionary Committee. He cannot consent to any interference but from the Bishop![66]

In July 1856, Prescott printed an 18-page pamphlet addressed "To the inhabitants of Ascension Parish, Carroll County," which articulated his theological position. In it Prescott speaks of the apostolic function and authority of a bishop, and of the three orders of the ministry described in the Bible. Because the Bishop is soon to come to Ascension Parish for confirmation, Prescott rebukes "among us those who will look coldly on our Bishop, and consider that they have no part nor lot in the rite he comes to administer and perhaps deny its authority as they deny his." The pamphlet then proceeds to defend the rite, citing Acts 8 and 19 and Hebrews 6: 1 & 2. Prescott explains that the Holy Ghost is given in baptism for regeneration and in confirmation for sanctification. He concludes, by speaking about the Real Presence of Christ on our altars.[67]

Finally, in March 1857 he is considering undertaking work of a missionary character in New York City. Bishop Potter of New York writes Bishop Whittingham that Prescott has said he would not seek a transfer from Maryland without his Bishop's free consent. Prescott has indicated to Bishop Potter that his father is anxious to have him nearer to him. On April 1, 1857 Prescott submitted his resignation to the Vestry of Ascension Church. And on the same day, Bishop Potter accepted Prescott's letter dimissory, confessing to Bishop Whittingham that he did not feel particularly easy about having Prescott in his diocese.[68]

The ministry which Prescott hoped to undertake in a part of New York City which bordered on Dr. Eigenbrodt's parish apparently failed to develop. On March 6, 1858 Prescott wrote Bishop Whittingham from Boston in a despairing mood.[69] He wonders whether he should renounce the ministry since the Church has not been able or willing to provide him a place in which to exercise that ministry. Once again the good Bishop comes to Prescott's aid. On July 12, 1858 Prescott writes from New Haven that he has heard from Mr. Archer, inviting him to become the Chaplain of the Patapsco Institute and to serve the Church at Ellicott's Mills (now Ellicott City). Prescott is uncertain whether in his father's present condition it is not his duty to remain in New Haven.[70]

MARYLAND: ST. PETER'S CHURCH & THE PATAPSCO INSTITUTE, ELLICOTT'S MILLS

On March 16, 1858, the Reverend Dr. Harry Croswell died in his 80th year. While Dr. Croswell had not mentioned Oliver Prescott in his Diary for several years before his death, still his death removed one more trusted friend from Oliver's life. Dr. Croswell had been pastor at Trinity Church all of Oliver Prescott's life.

The Patapsco Institute was a fine boarding school for young ladies. The Vice Principal of the Institute was H. Katherine Van Bibber, the widow of Lucretia Van Bibber's brother, George. Perhaps the Van Bibbers of Westminster had put in a good word for Prescott. At any rate, the Bishop encouraged Prescott to accept the offer. On July 26 Prescott wrote Whittingham from New Haven. "I thank God that He has put it into your heart to recognize me as one ready for any work to which I may be led."[71] Prescott plans to leave New Haven at once so that he can take advantage of the vacation at the Institute to set going his parochial work. St. Peter's Church in Ellicott's Mills was organized in 1842. Bishop Whittingham had consecrated its brick building in 1854. Soon after arriving in Ellicott's Mills Prescott found that two women had been conducting a Sunday School for 40 to 50 children of mill workers in which they had been taught reading, writing, geography and such religion as they could.[72] He plans to bring these children to the Church and catechize them (with other scholars) every Sunday afternoon. Prescott also asks the Bishop's opinion of his conducting a missionary preaching service in a hall in the village preceded by the litany. In sum, everything looks encouraging there.

By November 3, the Sunday School has grown to 75 children whom Prescott catechizes every Sunday.[73] He has been requested to organize a Bible class for adults about which he says he knows nothing and for which he seeks the Bishop's guidance. Further, Prescott has taken steps towards a free night school for boys. Small wonder that he expresses the hope that this year will be the last in which one person will be obliged to do the work of two.

In May 1859, Prescott travels to New Haven to officiate at the wedding of his younger brother, William, and therefore asks to be excused from attending the Diocesan Convention. On June 20, 1859, back in Ellicott's Mills, Prescott informs the Bishop that all his life he has anticipated the pleasure of a trip abroad and a way now seems opened to his taking it.[74] Prescott has been asked to take a 16-year old youth named Charles H. Bredemyer to Europe. Bredemyer's father had died in 1850 leaving a substantial estate in trust for his widow and two children of whom Charles was the younger. The trustee of Charles' assets was Mr. John H. B. Latrobe.

Prescott took his vacation in August. While on holiday in Pittsfield, Massachusetts he wrote Bishop Whittingham expressing discouragement almost to desperation.[75] He has not been able to procure an assistant and doesn't know where he can find one. He does not see how he can endure the coming nine months of labor like those just past. Added to this, he continues to be haunted by the wretched certificate which he had signed in Massachusetts and he feels he ought to do something by way of a Memorial at the upcoming General Convention. The Bishop replied promptly, as usual. By August 29, Prescott is resolved to go back to work and do the best he can and leave the rest to God.[76] Nothing more was said about a Memorial to the General Convention. The Bishop apparently had dissuaded Prescott from that step.

On November 2, 1859 trouble was brewing. Mr. Robert H. Archer, the principal of the Patapsco Institute had invited the Rev. Dr. William Wyatt, the venerable Rector of Old St. Paul's Church in Baltimore, to baptize the Archer's infant in the Institute Chapel without consulting Prescott. Prescott was highly indignant at both Archer and Wyatt and wrote the Bishop to that effect.[77] Prescott hoped to be able to see the Bishop before the baptism took place. Evidently the Bishop was unable to placate Prescott or to persuade Dr. Wyatt and Mr. Archer to change their plans. In the following three months Prescott's relationship with Archer deteriorated to the point where on January 24, 1860 Archer wrote Prescott requesting his immediate and entire withdrawal from the Chaplaincy of the Institute.[78] Archer said that Prescott had made himself very objectionable to him and his family and has rendered himself unfit for his responsible duties. This last phrase angered Prescott who demanded an explanation or retraction from Archer. In forwarding to the Bishop his correspondence with Archer, Prescott considered Archer's charge false and libelous and not only his character but that of his priestly order was endangered by it.

Prescott submitted his resignation to the Bishop, who declined acting upon it, leaving the matter up to St. Peter's Vestry.[79] Archer submitted his resignation from the Vestry, but returned as soon as Prescott left St. Peter's. The Rev. Francis Lightbourn was engaged to serve St. Peter's Church for one year while Prescott was on leave of absence. Prescott's pastoral record book is preserved in the General Seminary Library. In it he records the members of the parish, prospective members, etc. Inside the back cover is the notation, not in Prescott's handwriting, "Rev. Mr. Prescott, Charles Bredemyer and Benj. Prescott left Elliott's Mills Feby. 17, 1860." Benjamin Prescott was Oliver's 16-year old nephew, the son of Oliver's oldest brother who had died in 1852. Benjamin was a whole orphan; his mother died when he was two years old. We don't know how long Benjamin had been living with his uncle Oliver in Ellicott's Mills. He was approximately the same age as Charles Bredemyer and probably provided some companionship for him.

The troubles with Mr. Archer reveal something of Prescott's personality. While he was extremely deferential toward those in authority over him (chiefly Bishop Whittingham), Prescott expected the same deference and respect from others. Was he short-tempered? Did the physical and emotional fatigue caused by his pastoral over-commitment cause him to lose control? The prudent thing for Prescott to have done would have been to welcome Dr. Wyatt to perform the Archer baptism. But where a principle was at stake, Prescott could be stubborn and inflexible. Did he feel he could make an issue of his pastoral prerogatives at this particular moment because he felt secure with the prospect of taking Bredemyer to Europe? We can only hold these conjectures in mind in the light of his past and future life.

EUROPE

Three letters which Prescott wrote from Europe have survived. The first dated June 15, 1860 from Milan is addressed to his sisters in New Haven.[80] It is labeled No. 12 and is a long, chatty description of his experiences in Northern Italy. He is greatly disappointed to have received no word from home in nearly six weeks. He is able to attend English service at the Hotel Grand Bretagne at Bellagio where there is an English Chaplain. He says that

> "Charles has been trying very hard to behave better and really I pity him for he is a most unfortunate animal. I don't have much to do with him and he has to find amusement as he best can, and with no resources in himself, no taste for fine scenery or beautiful walks, with no love for anything but low company and low amusements."

Prescott himself is giving five or six hours a day to French, he sleeps a good deal and walks about and smokes the rest of the time. He could feel much less homesick if he could hear from his family at home.

The second letter is dated July 9, 1860 and is addressed to Bishop Whittingham from Cadenabbia on Lake Como, Italy.[81] Prescott explains that he is ready and willing to return and work at any moment. He has informed Charles Bredemyer's guardian, Mr. Latrobe that he cannot continue in charge of Charles any longer and for him to make other arrangements for the young man. So far as St. Peter's Church is concerned, Prescott realizes that Mr. Lightbourn still has six months remaining on his contract as locum tenens there. In spite of this, Prescott proposes that he return to the parish and resume personal charge and active exercise of his rectorship, working together with Mr. Lightbourn. Prescott is sure that there is enough work for the two of them and also that means will be forthcoming to support both priests in the parish. Prescott concludes "trusting, my dear Bishop, that this will be the last trouble into which I shall drag you."

The third letter is dated July 22, 1860 and is addressed to his sisters from Berne, Switzerland.[82] Like his letter to them of June 15, it is long and includes many details of his travels. He and Charles have been on a walking tour of the Alps. He expects to be home in New Haven about the second week in October and hopes to vote for Stephen Douglas in the upcoming national election. He concludes that after six months of travel there he has given about all the time to Europe that he can spare. He has found that work is one of the best things to employ oneself with. He adds a postscript that he has received two letters from home after finishing this letter.

Apparently Bishop Whittingham did not think well of Prescott's proposal that he return to Ellicott's Mills and resume his rectorship there with Mr. Lightbourn's assistance. On November 5, 1860 Mr. T. Harwood Perine wrote Bishop Whittingham that the Vestry of the Church of the Redeemer in Baltimore had been unable to agree upon the choice of a rector and had engaged the services of the Rev. Mr. Prescott for five months and until the term of office of his substitute at Ellicott's Mills shall have expired.[83] Prescott's tenure at the Church of the Redeemer ended when it agreed to call the Rev. Mr. Stokes as its Rector. On January 8, 1861 Prescott wrote Bishop Whittingham of this development and that accordingly his work there is ending.[84]

RHODE ISLAND: TRINITY CHURCH, NEWPORT

On March 25, 1861 the Junior Warden of Trinity Church, Newport, Rhode Island wrote Bishop Whittingham informing him that Prescott had been serving that parish for the past two months during which time very many parishioners had become strongly attached to him and would like to call him as their rector at the Annual Parish Meeting after Easter.[85] The parish had been without a rector for a year and the Warden, Charles Hunter, fears that some of the Corporators, mindful of Prescott's troubles in Boston years ago, will oppose his election. Accordingly, Hunter asks for a private letter from the Bishop saying all he can in Prescott's favor in order to bolster support for him at the Annual Parish Meeting. Hunter concludes by speaking of Prescott's "ability, earnestness, zeal and entire fitness for the situation." We do not know how Trinity Church learned about Prescott. Perhaps he met someone from the parish during his travels in Europe who proposed his name to the Vestry.

A letter which Prescott wrote to his sister (presumably Mary) in New Haven on the second Sunday in Lent of 1861 gives us a picture of his life and ministry early in his stay at Newport.[86] Having had two services at Trinity Church that morning, he is to have a third service there that evening. His Lenten services have been well attended. The previous Friday evening which is his "lecture night," the Bishop of Rhode Island was also in town giving a lecture. Prescott's audience was only down about a dozen persons while the Bishop's lecture room was only half full. Prescott hopes to go to England in two years. He is paying $12 a week board which keeps him "pretty low on funds." But he hopes his salary will be increased soon (presumably when his position there was regularized) or that he can find cheaper lodgings.

On May 21, Prescott writes Whittingham informing him that he has, in fact, been called to the Rectorship of Trinity Church for one year.[87] The Annals of Trinity Church show that the vote to call Prescott received 41 affirmative votes and 28 negative.[88] The salary is to be $1,500 per annum. The divided vote explains Prescott's unwillingness to accept the call, "coming in the way it does." But he has agreed to do duty there until he comes to a decision. Weighing against accepting is the troubled condition of the parish which is polarized into several factions and has been without a rector for a year. Further, he seriously objects to Thomas Clark, the Bishop of Rhode Island. Prescott asks Bishop Whittingham to give him a letter dimissory to Rhode Island which he can present if he deems it necessary.

In this letter Prescott also mentions "my own personal perplexities in regard to my duty in the matter of my engagement of marriage which made me desirous of leaving Maryland for a while." This is the only mention in all the extant documents pertaining to Prescott of the possibility of marriage. Nothing further is known of the nature of the engagement or the person to whom he was engaged.

A month later Prescott writes Bishop Whittingham requesting an appointment with him in Baltimore and informing him that he has made no use of the letter dimissory.[89] On August 9 at a Vestry meeting in Trinity Church, Newport, Prescott accepts the invitation extended on Easter Monday to become its Rector.[90] Prescott reserves to himself the right of resignation thereof whenever it may seem to him expedient. Also at this Vestry meeting a letter was read from Bishop Clark informing the Vestry that he and the Standing Committee had reversed their previous decision and had given permission for the formation of a fourth parish in Newport to be called All Saints, to which Trinity's Vestry had objected. This new parish was controlled by Dr. A. G. Mercer, Trinity's immediate past rector. This suggests some of the tensions in Newport among various lay and clergy factions.

The very next day Prescott's father, Major Enos Alling Prescott, died in New Haven at the age of 74. As was customary at the time, his funeral was held at his home, 13 Whiting Street.[91] Two of his older sons, Benjamin and Enos had predeceased their father. Major Prescott was survived by his widow, Mary (always known in the family as "Polly"), a son, Harry who continued to direct the family shipping and coal business, Oliver, William and Frank, the youngest son, as well as his daughters Mary (also known as "Polly") and Emily. Major Prescott left an estate appraised at $28,309, not much greater than his father's estate 22 years before. His oldest surviving son, Harry, was executor of the estate.[92]

On September 6, Prescott writes Whittingham commiserating with him on his illness and inviting the Bishop to come to Newport to recuperate.[93] While Prescott is "not at housekeeping" himself, he assures the Bishop that he could be quite comfortable at the Aquidneck House. Prescott does not mention his own recent bereavement.

Evidently the Bishop did not accept Prescott's invitation. On October 15 Prescott wrote Whittingham to share letters which he had just received from both Ascension parish and St. Peter's Church in Maryland offering him the charge of the churches in those places.[94] Prescott assures the Bishop that his desire to return to Maryland is very sincere partly because he prefers the ecclesiastical atmosphere there and partly because he thinks he may be of some service to the Bishop "in the great trouble the burden of which falls so heavily upon your shoulders." This may allude to the Civil War which began when Ft. Sumter was fired upon on April 12, 1861. Maryland, a border state, had organized military forces fighting on both the Union and the

Confederate sides. Prescott concludes by saying that he has steered Trinity Parish through a sad season of dissension. He would be willing to accept the rectorship of Trinity Church if put in a position to deal strongly with the "self-willed troublers of the Church's peace." His only desire, he writes, is to do his duty and to have the strength to sacrifice personal feelings.

The same week, Dr. J. D. Ogden writes Bishop Whittingham from Newport.[95] Ogden is the son-in-law of Clement C. Moore with whom the Bishop served on the faculty of General Seminary in New York. Moore is now 83 years old, a summer resident of Newport, and a pew owner in Trinity Church. Ogden explains that the election of a rector in Rhode Island is the prerogative of the Corporators or pew owners, with proxies permitted. Prescott is universally respected and admired, Ogden says, but there are individuals who, for party motives, would oppose any permanent settlement of the parish's difficulties. Ogden requested a few lines from the Bishop expressing his opinion of Prescott which, in an emergency, might be quoted or referred to.

In mid November, Prescott wrote Whittingham a long discursive, personal letter which provides insight into Prescott's character and thinking.[96] He refuses to play politics in Trinity Church and to finesse a call as its rector. Apparently Bishop Whittingham has asked Prescott to consider coming to Baltimore to serve Mt. Calvary Church there, the Bishop's own family parish. Prescott replies:

> As regards Mt. Calvary or any other Church in any large
> city, I must feel very differently from what I now do ever to
> give one consideration. I know myself well enough not to
> be wise to the fact that it is better for me (better as I find it)
> to be subject to the petty curiosity, oversight and gossip of

a village or town, than the each-one-stand-his-own-business freedom of a city.

He then adds that:

"Whenever I get seriously at work I am more and more wearied with searchings of heart in regard to my old trouble in Massachusetts. It is now almost ten years since it occurred and the older I grow the more I wonder that so great a piece of tyranny was permitted . . . I have been condemned for a fault I never committed, and till I am loosed and let go free Satan certainly has an advantage over us.

Prescott concludes that in the Parish of Trinity Church he is successful. "There is a latent churchly element which meets me gladly. Besides, I have gathered it in from the whole city."

Shortly thereafter, Prescott sends Whittingham a draft of an Order of Prayer for Sunday Schools.[97] He requests the Bishop's imprimatur because he believes that as a presbyter he does not have the right to set forth an office for public use.

On February 7, 1862 at an adjourned meeting or the Corporation of Trinity Church, Prescott was elected rector.[98] On April 21, 1862 at the Easter Monday annual meeting of the Corporators, it was moved that the meeting of February 7 be declared illegal because no quorum was present. This resolution lost by 1 vote (that of the chairman). At an adjourned meeting of the Corporators on May 5 it was moved that because the Corporators are divided as to the propriety of calling Oliver S. Prescott to be the permanent pastor of the parish, it would be unwise to call any minister who could not command an almost unanimous vote of the Corporators and congregation. This resolution was tabled. At this meeting a letter from Prescott dated April 5, 1862 was received and recorded in which he declared himself the Rector of Trinity Church by his own act and by the Corporation's election. Prescott appended two conditions: 1) that he not be called upon to be instituted as rector and 2) that he have the right to resign at any moment, however soon, when he shall consider such an act consistent with his duty to God and His Church. A motion to appoint a committee to nominate a minister was indefinitely postponed and the Corporation moved to confirm the whole action of the meeting of February 7 which carried by a vote of 39 to 34, an even narrower margin than that of the previous year. Certified copies of the minutes of the meetings of February 7 and April 21 (the Annual Meeting) and May 5 were to be sent to the Bishop, the Standing Committee of the Diocese and the Rector. So the stalemate appeared to have been ended at last, although the deep division in the Corporation continued which did not bode well for Prescott.

Weary of the whole business, Prescott wrote Whittingham on April 22 that he believed the time had come when duty to the Church would permit him to decline the invitation to become Rector of Trinity Church.[99] He again offers himself to Whittingham and asks for work in his Diocese.

But work was not forthcoming from Maryland. Instead, in the summer of 1863, he receives an appointment as chaplain to serve the nearby military hospital at Portsmouth Grove, which he deemed it his duty to accept. Prescott agreed to continue filling the pulpit of Trinity Church while serving as chaplain.[100] According to a clipping in his file at Trinity College, Hartford, Prescott served as a U.S. Army hospital chaplain from July 4 to September 29, 1862.[101]

For many years it had been the custom for the Vestry of Trinity Church to distribute to poor and needy persons the communion alms from the service on Christmas. This was clearly in violation of canon law which specified that communion alms should be deposited with the minister of the parish and distributed at his discretion. Prescott informed the parish of this canon before the Christmas Eucharist and he proceeded to take the communion alms for distribution himself. The Vestry met on December 26 to discuss this change in their usual procedure. Prescott was sick and not able to attend this meeting, but he sent the Vestry a long, carefully worded, polite but firm, letter explaining why he had handled the Christmas communion alms in this way.[102] He appealed to mutual respect for the canon law of the Church as the best and proper way for them to work together. He asked that this letter be placed on the records of the Vestry's December 26 meeting.

Matters moved rapidly thereafter. At its December 26 meeting the Vestry received Prescott's letter and referred the matter to a committee of three to report at an adjourned meeting on January 2, 1863.[103] At the January 2 meeting, the Vestry voted to return Prescott's letter of December 26 to him. They requested him to tell the Vestry the amount of the Christmas offering, to whom and in what amounts to each individual it had been distributed so that the Vestry could appropriately distribute other funds in their hands for the relief of the poor. On January 13, Prescott wrote the Vestry that his disposition of the Christmas alms was made with the advice of the Senior Warden. He then invited the Vestry to name one of its members with whom he would share in confidence any information about the alms that person might desire. Anything further Prescott considered would be a breach of professional propriety which he refused to perpetrate.

The Vestry replied by inviting Prescott to meet with them the next evening, January 14, to help them distribute the remaining funds available for the poor. At the meeting, Prescott declines further discussion of the matter with the Vestry and he informs them that he has decided to lay the matter with all documents before the Corporation sometime between this date and Easter Monday. At a Special Meeting of the Corporation on January 16, Prescott announced his intention to resign at the Annual Meeting on Easter Monday to take effect ten days after the acceptance of election by his successor as rector. On February 5, Prescott tells the Vestry that he has, in fact, distributed the Christmas offerings strictly in accord with the canons of the Church and he declines having anything further to say on the subject. The Vestry repeats its request for an accounting as it had done at its January 2 meeting.

At the Annual Meeting, Prescott's formal letter of resignation is submitted to take effect ten days after he is informed of his successor's acceptance. On July 20, 1863, a successor is elected rector of Trinity Parish and on July 30 Prescott ends his connection with the Parish. He notes that during the first 26 months of his tenure there he has baptized 28 persons, presented 18 persons for confirmation, married 8 couples, and buried 44 individuals. When he arrived, there were 199 parishioners to who were added 142 persons during his time of service. While 51 persons had died or were removed, making a final total of 290 communicants. The editor of the Parish Annals notes that many of those added were persons who had been members of Trinity Church for years, but whose names through the neglect of the previous rector had not been recorded. It was typical of Prescott's ministry in this and other parishes he served to prepare complete and accurate parish membership lists.

Prescott was a man who stuck to his conviction and principles even if doing so was personally costly to him. Had Prescott grown weary of coping with the factions in Trinity Parish? Perhaps. The fact that he wrote Bishop Whittingham in April, eight months before the communion alms crisis broke informing the Bishop that the time had come when duty would permit him to decline the rectorship of Trinity, suggests that he was ready to leave long before he resigned. Trinity Parish was the largest, oldest, wealthiest, and most prestigious parish that Prescott had ever served. His salary of $1,500 was several times greater than any he had received hitherto. If worldly ambition or personal comfort had been important to him, he might have been willing to compromise his convictions in his dealings with the Vestry. But he would not and he did not. He left without another clerical post in hand. But he trusted God to provide.

Shortly before leaving Newport in July 1863, Prescott delivered a sermon in Trinity Church entitled, "The Power of the Resurrection," on the Sunday following the funeral of the Rev. Clement Clark Moore. The sermon was published in Newport with two letters to Dr. Moore from Bishop H. C. Potter of New York.[104]

CONNECTICUT: CHRIST CHURCH, WEST HAVEN

In mid-October 1863, Prescott was in Westminster, Maryland. His visit there may have been to explore the possibility of his returning to Ascension parish as its rector. Certainly he went to Maryland to visit Grafton, who was still serving as assistant to the Reverend William Wyatt, at St. Paul's Church, Baltimore. On November 2, the Rev. James

Chrystal wrote Bishop Whittingham charging Prescott and Grafton with belief in transubstantiation, praying to the Virgin Mary and other saints and concluding that he does not feel Prescott is a fit person to succeed him at Ascension parish.[105] According to Chrystal, Prescott said that Papal Supremacy was the only peculiarly Latin doctrine which he did not believe. It may be that Chrystal's attack on Prescott's theology eliminated any support which there may have been in Ascension parish to call Prescott as rector.

On January 11, 1864, Prescott's mother died at the age of 75. Her funeral, like that of her husband, was held from the family home at 13 Whiting Street, New Haven.

The first half of 1864 Prescott assisted the Right Reverend Horatio Southgate, who was rector of Zion Church in New York City. Bishop Southgate, who had earlier been Bishop in Constantinople, succeeded William Croswell as rector of the Church of the Advent in 1852. So he and Prescott knew each other at the time of Prescott's trials in Massachusetts. In 1864, Prescott published a sermon entitled, "The Benedicite: A Hymn of Praise to the Triune God."[106] This sermon, which Prescott preached in Zion Church on the first Friday in Lent, 1864, he dedicated to Bishop Southgate. In the New York Diocesan Journal for 1864, Prescott reports that on the first Sunday in July he terminated his connection with Bishop Southgate and since then has done no public official act in the Diocese requiring record.

In December 1864, Prescott and Grafton made a long retreat in an old shack on the south coast of Fire Island, New York. Grafton has left a detailed account of this retreat which is surely one of the first of its kind in the life of the American Episcopal Church.[107]

The two men spent their mornings in prayer and study and did their own household chores. During the retreat, a U.S. Coast Guard cutter noticed a light and activity in this remote spot and came ashore suspecting Confederate spies. Fortunately, the two priests could produce a letter from the Reverend Morgan Dix, rector of Trinity Church in New York, who was known to the Navy officer. Apart from the excitement of this encounter, the retreat was an important turning point for both Prescott and Grafton, who both resolved to pursue the religious life in community in England. They returned to their homes in time for Christmas; Prescott to New Haven and Grafton to Baltimore. The following spring, Grafton left St. Paul's Church in Baltimore and went to England to discuss with Church leaders there the possibility of establishing an Anglican religious community for men.

But Prescott did not go to England with Grafton. Instead, he continued living in New Haven with his family. And he started working in the Church of the Nativity in Bridgeport, Connecticut. This parish had been established on the outskirts of Bridgeport by a wealthy businessman, E. Ferris Bishop.[108] Bishop had a vocation to the ordained ministry and was ordained deacon in 1860 and priest three years later by the Bishop of Connecticut. Bishop was president of three railroads and chief executive officer of the highly successful Bridgeport Steamboat Company. He was the patron of the Church of the Nativity and had erected for it a fine stone building with an adjacent building to house several clergy. The church was consecrated by Bishop Williams on January 15, 1859. He was not, however, its rector. That post was filled by the elderly Reverend Dr. G. S. Coit, who was its titular rector. Dr. Coit had for 28 years been the rector of St. John's Church in Bridgeport, until October 1861. In the 1866 Connecticut Diocesan Journal, Mr. Bishop reported that Prescott had assisted at the Church of the Nativity without remuneration all the previous year.

On March 6, 1866 Prescott wrote Bishop Whittingham to say that Bishop Quintard of Tennessee had offered him a parish in Nashville, which Prescott has accepted on condition that it is renewed after Quintard has seen Whittingham and learned "what manner of man I am."[109] Prescott suspects that Quintard may not want Prescott in his diocese when he learns that his reputation is "tainted with the charge of a leaning towards Catholicism." At the same time, Prescott admits that it would be very pleasant to find himself again under Episcopal care and "to give up being a presbyterian." Evidently nothing came of the offer and Prescott continued assisting at the Church of the Nativity in Bridgeport.

Then, on July 31, Prescott met Bishop Williams and later that day carefully drafted a letter to follow up on that personal conversation.[110] Prescott must have felt this letter of sufficient importance so that he saved his draft of it for many years. Apparently, what precipitated the interview and subsequent letter was Bishop Williams' receipt of Prescott's letter dimissory from the Diocese of New York. Williams was reluctant to accept the letter dimissory for a priest who had no clerical appointment in his Diocese. And he was also reluctant to give consent to Prescott's accepting a post at the Church of the Nativity. Indeed, in March of that same year, Williams had written Mr. Bishop rebuking him mildly for ceremonies at the Church of the Nativity.[111]

Prescott explains in his letter to Bishop Williams that his actual residence is in Connecticut because he has not the means of living elsewhere. Prescott is willing to have Bishop Williams return his letter dimissory to New York and for it to remain there until such time as Bishop Potter is compelled to act on it. (There were so few able-bodied clergy without cures in the 19th Century that bishops were not sure how to deal with them.) Prescott continues by expressing his personal liking for Bishop Williams since they first met at what was then Washington College in Hartford the summer after Prescott enrolled. Prescott says he shall never forget how Williams then personally "took captive my boys heart." Prescott states, "I have got to live and I have got to live as a priest of the P.E. Church, more than this, so far as I can see, I have got to do this in Connecticut." It would grieve him to go to Bridgeport without Williams' blessing. Prescott is weary of notoriety. He would like to change his name and tuck his face under a cowl—but Prescott strikes out those words. Prescott concludes:

> Should I come into your Diocese it would not be to found a community, but because I cannot live elsewhere and because to my mind the canons require that I must also live here canonically.

Apparently, Bishop Williams dropped his objections because Prescott continued assisting at the Church of the Nativity, although unofficially and without remuneration.

Meanwhile, Grafton is writing Prescott from London urging him to join him there.[112] Grafton knows that Prescott's "heart is all aglow" for the religious life which he has desired over and over again. Then, in lawyer-like fashion, Grafton marshals his arguments. First, there are hundreds of other priests who can serve his parish, but "if God has called you to the religious life, etc., that settles it." Second, family duties. If Prescott gives his sisters his share of his inheritance, they should be able to manage because they are good managers. Third, so far as money for the passage to England is concerned, if you do not have it, I will be responsible, Grafton writes. Anyway, wouldn't Prescott be justified in taking $400 or $500 from his inheritance for this purpose? Surely, the sale of the furniture, pictures and books might raise some cash. And possibly your congregation might make Prescott a purse. (Grafton must not have realized that with his many moves, Prescott could not have accumulated much in the way of household furnishings.) Finally, Grafton speaks of men in England who are leading holy lives who "in ritual (are) far ahead of the high and dry and what we see in America and whose acts at the altar, etc., are all we would ask." Grafton concludes that "we must not be monks, but a modern order. The ancient spiritual life embodied for work by the wisdom and experience of the church."

Grafton's appeal does not succeed. Writing from London on July 17, 1865, Grafton is pleased that from his letters Prescott is in good spirits and well.[113] Grafton then describes Brother Ignatius, whose flamboyant style repelled Grafton. Grafton sends the names of various makers of mass vestments and their cost for Mr. Bishop who wants them for the Church of the Nativity. But, Grafton asks, "is America ripe for them?" He advises that it is good to begin by using linen vestments and then to add colored stoles. Mindful of Prescott's ebullience about the Catholic revival, Grafton advises, "Don't herald it in newspapers. Don't report your services. Don't attract attention, which is unspiritual." Grafton then confides:

> "If God will, very quietly indeed in the autumn, some persons will get together and the work be begun." . . . (We) will meet at a place near Oxford, Mr. Benson's parish, and commence living by Rule and receiving instructions in the spiritual life and rules of a community. One will act as Superior (Mr. Benson probably) . . . The formation of the fuller rule will not be made till after a year.

Thus began what was to become the Society of St. John the Evangelist.

Prescott is still troubled by the certificate he signed for Bishop Eastburn and has asked Grafton to consult leading clergymen in England about the matter. Grafton has dutifully put the matter to Pusey, Neale, Liddon and Benson, who all agree and repeat the opinion which Prescott has heard before many times: what a bishop can impose a bishop can undo. Indeed, Dr. Neale considers a promise contrary to the faith to be void <u>ab initio</u>.

Apparently, Mr. Bishop is eager for the fledgling monastic community to settle at the Church of the Nativity. Grafton counsels:

> I think you can make Mr. Bishop understand that in a work
> so momentous as that of a brotherhood, requiring so much
> of discipline, the worst of all mistakes is precipitancy . . . If
> Mr. Bishop is desirous of our taking his place, he must be
> content (if it is at all dependent on me) to wait.[114]

Near the end of this very long letter Grafton declares that "E.B.P. (Edward Bouverie Pusey) wants Catholic truth brought home to intellectual Boston." It was a prophetic hope!

On November 3, 1865, Grafton wrote Prescott, "I am still waiting to hear from you and know you are proceeding in the best way and will let me know when the time comes."[115] On February 7, 1866 Grafton from Cowley again inquires:

> Will you not write me a letter and tell me (1) how you feel
> about coming out here for a short time. (2) Whether you

are still of the same mind about going in together for the formation of a religious order.[116]

On February 21, 1866, again writing at Cowley, Grafton continues in the same vein:

> If you have duties to your sisters, and if your lot is to care for and protect them, God will help you to do it and can bless us wherever we are and in what ever part of the vineyard we toil. But if it is not necessary and your duty, come with us.[117]

In spite of Grafton's repeated pleas to join him in England, Prescott's life took a surprising turn. On May 1, 1866 he became Rector of Christ Church in West Haven, Connecticut, at an annual salary of $400.[118] Christ Church was the second oldest parish in the Diocese, having been established in 1723. But it was still small and barely able to support a priest in 1866. When he arrived, Prescott could find only 53 communicants. West Haven itself was a community of farmers and fishermen, with a popular resort hotel on Long Island Sound. Its modest frame building was the oldest still in use in the Diocese. With his customary zeal, Prescott threw himself into the life of this parish.

Mindful of the problems which had arisen in Trinity Church, Newport over the disposition of special offerings, early in his ministry at West Haven, Prescott raised this issue which the parish referred to the Bishop and his advisors. On September 6, 1866, the Standing Committee of the Diocese concurred in Bishop Williams' decision that "on all occasions when the Holy Communion is administered, the offertory is in the hands and at the disposal of the Rector." Apparently, the Bishop was aware of the tensions which had risen in Newport between Prescott and his Vestry because the Bishop added that:

> The Rector of a Parish should exercise the right which common consent and usage have given him, and the Parish should also exercise their right, with such regard to the interests of the Parish and the church, and with such Christian courtesy and common sense, as will prevent any conflict of rights or duties between them.

The Bishop went on to say that "according to long-continued and general usage, the Rector may at any time make a collection for any specified object connected with the Parish or the Church at large." The Parish itself also had this right, as did the Diocese for collections for Diocesan purposes. This policy decision was spread on the pages of the 1867 Diocesan Journal.

This policy statement had wider implications for parish funding than might at first appear. In the 18th Century, in places such as Connecticut, where the Congregational Church was established as the State Church, local congregations were funded by a tax levied against each resident's property as recorded on the assessor's grand list. Members of other churches (such as Episcopalians) then asked that their church tax be remitted to their own parish, a request which was usually, but not always, granted. When, after the War of Independence, church and state were separated (which did not occur in Connecticut, for example, until 1818), this method of funding local parishes was no longer possible. At that time, the practice of annually auctioning church pews began. The best pews went to the highest bidders and it was customary for pews to have doors. Persons too poor to rent a pew, as well as occasional visitors, were required to sit in unrented pews in undesirable locations in the Church (such as the back corners) or in the gallery, if the church had one, or to stand in the aisle. The Tractarians early opposed the practice of auctioning pews and advocated what they called "free churches," that is, churches where worshippers were free to sit wherever they wished, first come first served. The problem with this principle was that the Holy Communion was the only service in which the Prayer Book provided for an offertory but the principal Sunday service was Morning Prayer which had no such provision (and still has none). The policy decision of 1866 in Connecticut made it officially possible to add an offering to the services of Morning and Evening Prayer and thereby the weekly offering of money could become the principal means of funding parishes. The auctioning of pews which was discriminatory on the basis of wealth and which was also a poor missionary strategy, gradually died out during the balance of the 19th Century. With this policy decision, Prescott instituted the weekly offertory at Christ Church, West Haven.

During the summer of 1866, Prescott moved to enlarge the old Church building. It was built between 1740 and 1742 and had become greatly dilapidated by the 19th Century. In 1840 and 1841, it was repaired and in 1842 Bishop Brownell consecrated the building at which service the Reverend Harry Croswell preached the sermon. (Trinity Church in New Haven had contributed generously to the building's repair.) In 1851, the building was lengthened and a shallow chancel five feet deep added. This was the edifice as Prescott found it. He drew up plans, which are still in the parish archives, to add a tower to the west end of the building and to lengthen the chancel. The tower contained a vestibule on the first floor, a meeting room above (off the rear gallery) and a belfry. A "good toned 800 lb. bell" was given as well as an organ. A small "transept" was added to the north side of the building for the choir and organ and a cross was placed on top of the tower, all enhancing the "churchly" appearance of the building. The cross on top of the tower shocked some folk in the town, some of whom promptly climbed up and removed it! The total cost of these improvements was about $1,200.

In Lent 1867, Prescott preached a series of sermons on the Four Last Scenes in our Divine Lord's Life, one of which on "The Cross of Christ" he published.[119] It is dedicated "To the Fathers of St. John the Evangelist, and, among them, to One Especially, to Whom the Author Owes More Than Can Be Told," a clear allusion to Charles Grafton. The tender quality of Prescott's dedication of this sermon indicates the affectionate bond between him and Grafton. The tone of Grafton's letters to Prescott from England suggests that that relationship was mutual. For example, Grafton wrote from Cowley on Feb. 21 1866 "And dear Oliver, I would kneel down before you and tell you all my sins, and you must know how long and heavy the catalogue is."

The enlarged church building was solemnly dedicated by the Bishop on the Feast of St. Simon and St. Jude (October 28, 1867), at which time seven persons were confirmed. This was Prescott's last service at West Haven, he having resigned as of November 1 of that year. In his final report, published in the 1867 Diocesan Journal, Prescott reported about 65 families, 77 communicants, 6 Sunday School teachers, and 25 scholars. During the year past he had officiated at one marriage and 2 burials. It was an impressive achievement in just eighteen months.

On December 27, 1866, the feast day of St. John the Evangelist, the Reverends Richard M. Benson, Simeon W. O'Neill, and Charles C. Grafton made their religious professions as Mission Priests of St. John the Evangelist. They all took the three-fold vows of poverty, chastity, and obedience. Benson, who was Vicar of the Church of St. John the Evangelist at Cowley where the young community was based, was the Superior. By the following October, Grafton was in the United States trying to recruit men for the brotherhood.[120] But he found none. He had two long conversations with Bishop Whittingham, who was much opposed to the present ritualistic movement. Grafton was successful in recruiting two women to join the Clewer Sisterhood in England. Baltimore was out of the question at present as a possible site for their brotherhood because of the Bishop's opposition. Grafton writes further to Prescott, "As you are already under a vow of celibacy, you have only to live up to it. You cannot go back from that, and entering an order will aid you to keep it." He feels it would be useless to attempt establishing any community in the United States without four persons to begin with.

Finally, sometime early in 1868, Prescott left for England to enter the novitiate of the Society. It had taken Prescott three full years from the time of his retreat on Fire Island to act on the decision he had made there and to leave for England. Did he delay in order to save enough money from his modest income to defray the cost of his passage? It is more likely that he found it very difficult to separate himself from the home and family in New Haven to which he had returned so frequently since his ordination. As Grafton had observed, Prescott had long lived as a celibate priest. He had also lived in or very near poverty. The salaries he earned in his several parishes, except for Trinity Church, Newport, were invariably minimal.

In the twenty years since his ordination as a deacon and his departure for England, Prescott had lived and served in many places. His longest tenure was thirty months at Trinity, Newport. So far as his ability to hold a position is concerned, Prescott was not stable. By contrast, Grafton held two positions in the same Diocese during his ten years in the ministry before leaving for England. Grafton had graduated from Harvard Law School. Prescott had attended both Trinity College (as it is now) and Yale but graduated from neither. Although they were close friends, the differences between them were striking. Prescott was hot tempered and volatile. Grafton even-tempered and prudent. Both were ritualistic, Anglo-Catholic priests. Both had a vocation to the monastic life. Prescott was widely known, even notorious, in the Episcopal Church, while Grafton was probably little known outside the Diocese of Maryland and the city of Boston where he was born.

ENGLAND: THE SOCIETY OF ST. JOHN THE EVANGELIST, COWLEY

Sometime in the first months of 1868, Prescott at long last went to England and entered the novitiate at Cowley near Oxford. His presence at the parish Church of St. John the Evangelist brought to four the number of priests in the community resident there: Fr. Benson, the parish vicar and superior of the community, Grafton and O'Neill, all professed members, and Prescott, a novice. The community consisted of two Englishmen and two Americans. We can fix the date of Prescott's entry into the community by a letter he wrote to Bishop Whittingham from Cowley dated March 8, 1868.[121] In it Prescott writes:

> Your kindness in the past is beyond all possibility of adequate
> thanks. Looked back upon from this distance it seems as if it
> were at one time, under God, the only bond which held me

(in) the way of salvation. You never will know in this world all you have been to me.

On November 12, 1869 Dr. George C. Shattuck wrote Bishop Whittingham from England that he had lately met two of the Bishop's former clergy now known as Father Grafton and Father Prescott.[122] Shattuck adds that he had stayed at the Mission House on Marston Street in Oxford and went to a retreat there. Shattuck was Dean of Harvard Medical School and a member of the Church of the Advent in Boston. He was the founder of St. Paul's School in Concord, New Hampshire to which he gave his country estate as a site for the School which he also endowed.[123]

Prescott wrote his sister, Mary, from Cowley on February 6, 1870.[124] It seems that the Reverend E. Ferris Bishop had made an offer to Prescott to come to his church in Bridgeport. At first Prescott was very anxious to accept the invitation, but now he is indifferent to it. Prescott recognizes that until the community at Cowley is stronger in numbers, it cannot undertake work in the United States. He then explains to his sister that he and his colleagues are mission priests, not parochial clergy. Prescott then describes his heavy schedule of appointments in England:

> I am very busy and a good heap of work is piled up before me. I have only three leisure days between this and Easter, that is, only four days on which I am not engaged to preach and with but two exceptions from 3 to 5 times every day. The ten days before Ash Wednesday I am advertised to preach and make addresses just 50 times and the 30 days following

90 times and this exclusive of three missions and my Lent
work at All Saints.

But Prescott reassures his sister:

For the first time in my life I have found myself really at
work, with enough to do while there are but seven days in
the week and twenty-four hours in the day, and with generous
loving hearts all around me grace to have me do what I can.

On June 6, 1870, Prescott took life vows in the Society of St. John
the Evangelist at Cowley. As we have seen, he had been celibate since
his ordination. And most of the time since then he had lived at or near
the poverty level. Now these conditions of his life were formalized and
to them was added the vow of obedience to the Superior, the Reverend
Richard Meux Benson. From the account sent to his sister four months
before his profession, Prescott's life in the novitiate was anything but
contemplative!

With two members of the Community who were American citizens,
it was understandable that Fr. Benson hoped they would be able to
help establish an American branch of the Society. Accordingly, a few
months after his profession, Prescott was sent to St. Clement's Church,
Philadelphia, the first parish in America to receive the ministrations of
a professed Cowley father. St. Clement's Church was founded in 1855
and its present building consecrated in 1864. The Reverend Herman
G. Batterson became rector in 1869 and with him the Catholic revival
began in the parish.[125] Prescott's first stay at St. Clement's was relatively
brief. Early in 1871, he was called from Philadelphia to the Church of
the Advent in Boston.

Dr. Shattuck writing from Nassau to Bishop Whittingham in a letter dated only 1871 gives a picture of the life at the Church of the Advent at that time.[126] There are five services a day, all pretty well attended, he says. The Litany is said daily at noon and this service is attended by many ladies who cannot leave home earlier in the day. Prescott has the assistance of two other clergymen, Mr. Fay and Mr. Webb (Fay was the Rev. H. Warren Fay, who had been ordained by Bishop Horatio Potter of New York in 1865). The Church of the Advent was at that time located on Bowdoin Street in a former Congregational Church (which is now the location of the Church of St. John the Evangelist). Prescott continued serving the Church of the Advent through 1871.

Early in 1872, the Reverend Alfred A. Curtis left as Rector of Mt. Calvary Church in Baltimore to become a Roman Catholic. Mt. Calvary was Bishop Whittingham's own family parish and he was very concerned to find the right priest to serve it. On February 21, 1872, Dr. Shattuck wrote the Bishop, "Prescott is the man for Mt. Calvary."[127]

The next day, Shattuck wrote a long letter to Bishop Whittingham with a full and frank appraisal of Prescott.[128]

> I think Mr. Prescott one of the most injudicious and indiscreet men I ever knew. And he has a peculiar faculty of making himself appear worse than he is. Still he is earnest, self-denying, hard-working, accomplished, a remarkably good teacher and preacher and he has done very good work in Boston, He has not succeeded yet in crucifying the element of self in will or in conceit. The good Lord, however, uses much poorer tools than he is to bring about good results . . . (Prescott is) of much greater intellectual ability than either Grafton or (Arthur) Ritchie. He is one of the very best

preachers and readers I ever listened to. Moreover, I believe him perfectly <u>loyal</u> to the Church! . . . Since he has been with us, not one person has left the Church. He has been personally on very good terms with our Bishop.

"Our Bishop" was Manton Eastburn, now in his last years as Bishop of Massachusetts. Either Bishop Eastburn had mellowed in his old age, or Prescott was very forgiving, or possibly both had made possible this happy reconciliation. Dr. Shattuck's recommendation of Prescott was of no avail. Bishop Whittingham nominated the Reverend Joseph Richey to Mt. Calvary Church.

In November 1871, Grafton left England to take charge of the Church of the Nativity in Bridgeport which Fr. Benson envisioned as a good setting for the novitiate.[129] The two centers of the Society then were to be Bridgeport under Grafton and Boston under Prescott. There was, however, considerable interchange of personnel between the two centers as well as movement of members between England and the United States. The fathers returned to Cowley for the annual month-long retreat in the summer. In 1873, Fr. Prescott and Fr. Arthur Hall conducted a retreat at Eastborne in England. But by that fall, Fr. Hall was in charge of the house in Bridgeport. The Society's residence in Bridgeport lasted only about two years. They withdrew on Thanksgiving Day 1874, forced by the unwillingness of the Bishop of Connecticut, John Williams, to license Fr. Hall to officiate there. And also by the extravagant liturgical requirements of the Reverend E. Ferris Booth.

In December 1875, Prescott wrote from England to the Wardens and Vestry of St. Clement's Church in Philadelphia accepting their call to be their rector. And by February 1876, Fr. Prescott and the Reverend Basil W. Maturin S. S. J. E. were in residence in the parish.

In the summer of 1875, Prescott's younger sister, Emily, entered the novitiate of the Community of St. John the Baptist located in New York City. Her decision must have gratified Fr. Prescott.[130] She was received as a Second Order Novice and because of her age, did not go to the Mother House in Clewer, England for her training. In 1877, she was dedicated in the Second Order of the Community as Sister Emily Prescott. She was very helpful in running the House as clothes sister, or kitchen sister or bursaress. In 1881, the Second Order was given up and Sister Emily now became Sister Augustine (her middle baptismal name was "Augusta"). In 1882, she was professed as a Choir Sister and immediately became Assistant Superior. She died in January 1889 just before her 62nd birthday.

PENNSYLVANIA: ST. CLEMENT'S CHURCH, PHILADELPHIA

The ritual innovations of Catholic-minded clergy had become so disturbing to many clergy and lay persons in the Episcopal Church that finally in 1868 many memorials were sent to the General Convention praying the Convention "to establish and enforce uniformity in Divine Worship in all our Churches."[131] After lengthy deliberation it was deemed unwise to adopt a canon on the subject of Ritual. But the House of Bishops appointed a committee of five of its members "to consider whether any additional provision for uniformity by canon or otherwise is practicable and expedient." At the General Convention of 1871, this Committee submitted a lengthy report recommending that a long list of liturgical acts be prohibited and further limiting choral services and ecclesiastical vesture.

The General Convention of 1871 spent much of its time discussing this report and voting on various canonical proposals to enforce ritual uniformity. In the end it could agree on no more than a resolution condemning "all ceremonies, observances and practices which are fitted to express a doctrine foreign to that set forth in the authorized standards of this Church." The House of Bishops then issued a Pastoral Letter strongly condemning what was known as "Eucharistic Adoration."

These two actions in 1871 did not satisfy those in the Church who were opposed to ritual changes and therefore more memorials on the subject were sent to the 1874 General Convention. It finally succeeded after extended debate in amending Title I, Canon 20, "Of the Use of the Book of Common Prayer" to prohibit certain ritual practices and certain acts of eucharistic adoration. Finally, the bishops and the critics of high church ritual had a weapon to use which they hoped would enforce uniformity in public worship and banish ritual changes.

When Prescott wrote Bishop Williams of Connecticut requesting that his letter dimissory be sent to Bishop Stevens of Pennsylvania, he said:

> You know that Bishops (in America) are not so enamored of me that they receive me with much cordiality . . . I do not contemplate the severance of my connection with you without sincere regret. You won my boyish admiration. You have still my affection and esteem.[132]

Meanwhile, Prescott wrote to Bishop Stevens from Oxford on January 21, 1876 on the eve of his departure for America:

Someone has been good enough to send me a copy of a Philadelphia newspaper in which I am spoken of as the new Rector of St. Clement's Church and that Church is spoken of as, through me, coming under the control of the Society of St. John the Evangelist to which I have the honor to belong. Of course this is nonsense. The Parish of St. Clement's has not, necessarily any more connection with the SSJE because I am a member of it, than it has with my father's family because I am a member of that . . . My obedience to you is as full and will be as conscientiously given as if I were not a member of any Society at all.[133]

The newspaper's description of the relationship between Prescott, St. Clement's Church, the Society, and the Diocese of Pennsylvania hints at what was in due time to become a very serious problem, Prescott's easy dismissal of the matter to the contrary notwithstanding. This letter concludes with Prescott correcting another error. "I am not a graduate of Yale College, or of any other, though I was once a member of it."

In April 1876, Bishop Stevens wrote Prescott that he did not "purpose" to make any appointment for confirmation at St. Clement's Church.[134] This was the same tactic that Bishop Eastburn had used more than twenty years earlier in his dealings with the Church of the Advent in Boston. Prescott replied the next day regretting Bishop Steven's decision. On July 26, Bishop Stevens informed Prescott that he had accepted Prescott's letter dimissory from the Diocese of Connecticut.[135]

In October 1876, Prescott traveled to Montreal and conducted there a prolonged Prayer Meeting or Retreat, concluding by preaching at St.

John's Church on Sunday. The Bishop of Montreal, the Right Reverend Ashton Oxenden, promptly issued, on October 4, a letter inhibiting Prescott from officiating in the Diocese of Montreal with copies sent to the bishops of the Episcopal Church of America.[136] Prescott was understandably offended and responded with a fiery reply to Bishop Oxenden from Philadelphia on October 10. Three days later, Prescott sent to Bishop Stevens a copy of this letter.

This letter evidently led Bishop Stevens to call Prescott in to his office for a conversation on October 17. In the course of that meeting, the Bishop thought Prescott said that at daily celebrations of the Eucharist held in the Clergy House at St. Clement's, the Prayer Book service was not used in its entirety. The next day Bishop Stevens wrote Prescott requesting him to immediately discontinue such celebrations (apparently referring to certain omissions, not to the daily celebrations themselves). The Bishop also referred to Prescott's description of himself as "Curate of Cowley St. John's Church in the Diocese of Oxford." The Bishop informed Prescott that under the canons of the American Church, he could not at the same time be a Curate in the Diocese of Oxford and a Rector in the Diocese of Pennsylvania and he requested Prescott to decide in which Diocese he wished to be solely and canonically attached.[137]

The tone of Prescott's reply of October 19 was polite.[138] He asks the Bishop to tell him what the omissions and additions to the Communion Service are to which the Bishop alludes because he cannot recollect that they touched upon this subject in their conversation. He then protests his desire to conform to the doctrine, discipline and worship of the Episcopal Church. If he errs he promises to correct any mistake as soon as he is convicted of it. Prescott then says that he thought that in accepting election as Rector of St. Clement's Church he was committing himself to membership in the Diocese of Pennsylvania. The Bishop had recently inhibited Fr. Maturin from functioning in the Diocese of Pennsylvania. Prescott asks if this inhibition includes giving lectures or addresses in the school building on other occasions than those of public worship. He reminds the Bishop that he had sometime before asked permission to invite Fr. Benson of Oxford to officiate at St. Clement's during Benson's visit to Philadelphia. Finally, Prescott asks his Bishop for a copy of the letter which Stevens sent to the Bishop of Montreal which led him to inhibit Prescott there. Since the Canadian Bishop read Stevens' letter at a public meeting, Prescott assumes that the letter is no longer a confidential communication.

Bishop Stevens was upset by this letter which he found evasive and which did not comply with either of his requests.[139] For Prescott to be unable to recollect that they touched on the subject of omissions and additions to the Communion Service amazes the Bishop. He adds:

> It was a marked feature of that interview. Could I the next day write a letter to you largely based on that conversation and requiring you to do certain things in connection with the facts then stated, unless such a conversation had taken place, and unless it had made a deep impression on my mind? (The Bishop's emphasis)

Nor was the Bishop satisfied with Prescott's reply regarding his canonical membership in the Diocese of Pennsylvania. Stevens reiterates his request for Prescott to choose clearly between the Diocese of Oxford and Pennsylvania. The Bishop will consider Prescott's request regarding Fr. Benson's visit when Prescott has satisfactorily answered these two requests. Finally, Bishop Stevens makes it clear that his inhibition of Fr. Maturin covers all places, times, and services within the Diocese of Pennsylvania. He does, however, give permission to Maturin to administer the Holy Communion to a very aged and feeble lady <u>once</u> and in <u>private</u> (emphasis is the Bishop's).

In replying to this letter, Prescott on November 3 writes that he does not know of any omissions or additions (except for the longer exhortation) and that a letter from his Wardens and Vestry will inform him that they know of no such changes in the Communion Service either in the clergy house or in the chapel celebrations.[140] Finally, in a letter dated November 14 to his Bishop, Prescott says he is glad that one of the Bishop's requirements is so readily disposed of.[141] So far as the other request is concerned, Prescott says that he elects to retain the rectorship of St. Clement's Church and to reside in Philadelphia and therefore to have Bishop Stevens as his Diocesan. This correspondence between Prescott and the Bishop of Pennsylvania coming so soon after Prescott's settling at St. Clement's Church did not bode well for their future relationship.

On January 26, 1877 Prescott wrote Bishop Stevens to renew his invitation of eight months previous to visit St. Clement's in person for the purpose specified in the National Canons, namely to examine the state of the Church, the behavior of its clergy, to administer confirmation, to preach the Word of God, and possibly to celebrate the Lord's Supper.[142] Prescott concludes this brief letter saying:

> You will pardon me, if I do wrong in adding, that it seems to me most desirable, that you should know something of the ways and work of this important Parish, from personal observation.

The Bishop received this letter the following day after he had written "with real grief and pain" a long letter specifying ten points about which Prescott did not conform to the doctrine and worship of the Episcopal Church and officially requesting that Prescott discontinue these practices.[143] The list included, in sum: 1) All genuflections by clergy and choristers; 2) the use of candles other than those needed to read the service; 3) the use of a processional cross and all ceremonial processions; 4) the wearing by the clergy of vestments other than those specified; 5) the elevation of the communion elements during or after their Consecration; 6) mixing water with the wine in the chalice; 7) the use of acolytes in worship; 8) the dropping of the voice by the celebrant during part of the Communion service; 9) all prayers, sentences and hymns not authorized by the Book of Common Prayer; 10) the discontinuance of any omissions prescribed for Divine Service. It was essentially the same list that General Convention had considered in 1871 but had not included in the Ritual Canon 24 finally adopted in 1874. To this letter the Bishop added a note saying that when he had been informed of Prescott's compliance with these requests, he would then be able to make an Episcopal Visitation to St. Clement's Church.

Prescott replied on February 5 saying that if he were to comply with the Bishop's requests he would feel compelled to resign as Rector and that he did not believe his parishioners would accept his resignation or their right to worship God according to the dictates of their conscience.[144] Further, if Prescott does not comply and Bishop Stevens continues to refuse to visit the Parish, the matter in twelve months will have to be referred to a "Council of Conciliation" as required in the National Church canons. Prescott says further:

I still wish that you knew something of us from personal observation. There are the most mistaken and wild and absurd reports afloat in regard to us . . . Our services are not open to some of the practices to which you object.

He concludes:

As you decline to come to us, I shall be glad to wait upon you in company with my Warden and two Vestrymen, and we will give you direct and trustworthy information on any points you may see fit to bring before us.

The Bishop was very upset by Prescott's reply. Stevens writes on February 10 that he considers Prescott's letter "an evasion of present duty and such a subterfuge for present disobedience as unworthy the character of a Christian priest."[145] Nevertheless, Bishop Stevens complies with Prescott's requests and agrees to visit St. Clement's Church, accompanied by three gentlemen to meet with the Rector, Warden, and two Vestrymen "to examine the state of the Church" and "to inspect the behavior of its clergy." The Bishop pointedly omits officiating at confirmation or preaching or celebrating the Holy Communion. In other words, this is to be a private visit in the Vestry room of the Church.

The meeting took place on Saturday afternoon, February 17, 1877.[146] Accompanying the Bishop were the Reverend Dr. G. E. Hare, Mr. George C. Morris, and Mr. James S. Biddle. From St. Clement's were Henry Flanders, Warden, and William Pepper and Thomas J. Diehl, Vestrymen.

The Pennsylvania Diocesan Archives contain the Reverend Dr. Hare's summary of this visit. He thought that Prescott was adroit rather than straightforward; that he was not so much in sympathy with the Episcopal Church as in love with opinions and practices which this Church had abandoned; that he followed the right of private judgment to the extent of ignoring law both written and unwritten; and that he singularly mistook the puerile for the majestic. Mr. George C. Morris concluded that Prescott, while desiring to obtain the Bishop's approval had, at the same time, an avowed intention of maintaining an "advanced ritual" and of exercising the liberty of private judgment as to what was proper and allowable. Mr. Morris found Prescott's answers naturally guarded and defensive so as to avoid, if possible, hurtful admissions. Dr. Hare, however, found that Prescott acknowledged all usages they inquired of. The result of the visit was that ten days later the Bishop wrote Prescott reiterating his requests of January 27.[147] To this Prescott replied the next day reiterating <u>his</u> reasons for non-compliance as stated in his letter of February 5 and suggesting that the matter be referred immediately to a Council of Conciliation.[148]

The Vestry of St. Clement's was supportive of their Rector. They met on March 7 stating that the recent correspondence between Bishop Stevens and Fr. Prescott had been shared with them, and that the usages and ceremonies observed in the parish in the worship of Almighty God were dear to them. The Vestry, therefore, declared that it was their solemn conviction that the Rector should not accede to the demands made upon him by the Bishop and that a Council of Conciliation should be called which, hopefully, would vindicate the rights of the Parish. Finally, while deprecating the thought of turning to civil tribunals for settlement of these difficulties, still the Vestry recognized that such a course may be necessary.

The Bishop responded to this deadlock by referring the matter to the Standing Committee of the Diocese as his Council of Advice, on March 15. The Standing Committee advised the Bishop to give his "godly admonition" and "godly judgment" to require the discontinuance of the (ten) practices referred to in the Bishop's letter. A month later, on April 17, the Bishop, acting upon the advice of his Canonical Council, officially gave his admonition and judgment requiring Prescott to discontinue the practices referred to in his letter of January 27, 1877.[149] These practices the Bishop deemed to be "unauthorized, irregular and injurious to the peace and welfare of the Church."

Prescott was unable to reply to the Bishop's formal admonition until May 3 because he had been out of town for two weeks during which no letters were forwarded to him.[150] He promised only partial compliance to the Bishop's requests, viz. to discontinue omission of the Exhortation; any kneeling by the officiant from the end of the Prayer of Humble Access until after the Benediction; any dropping of the voice during the prayer of Consecration; any elevation of the Sacred Gifts with reference to the devotion of the people; the use of any prayers not taken from Holy Scripture or the Prayer Book; and all processions except on the great festivals. It was only a partial victory and quite unsatisfactory to the Bishop and those hoping to stamp out "Romish" rituals at St. Clement's Church.

In his reply of May 19, the Bishop lifted his inhibition against Fr. Maturin who was now canonically connected with the Diocese of New York and thus free to assist Prescott at St. Clement's.[151] The Bishop was unable to relax his requirements of Prescott and found his disobedience "thoroughly disloyal and unchurchly and a continuing great grievance in this Diocese." Therefore, he saw no necessity for further correspondence on this subject until Prescott is willing to comply with the Bishop's admonition and judgment.

On November 14, 1877, Prescott wrote Bishop Stevens requesting an autumn visitation and informing him that three members of the parish wish to become candidates for holy orders in other dioceses than Pennsylvania should the Bishop approve.[152] Within St. Clement's Church, Prescott's ministry was well received and supported. Needless to say, the Bishop refused to visit St. Clement's that fall.

Prescott wrote the Bishop on January 28, 1878 enclosing a clipping from the <u>Record</u> newspaper which included a quote from the Bishop.[153] Was the Bishop accurately quoted, Prescott asked? He then repeated his request that the Bishop schedule a spring visit to St. Clement's. On January 30, Bishop Stevens repeated his stand that he could not "complete his visit of February 17 last" (that is by confirming candidates and preaching) until Prescott complied with his official requests on April 17 last. So far as the quotation in the local newspaper, the Bishop holds himself responsible to no one for any alleged utterances of his found in public print. In any event, Prescott well knows the Bishop's opinion of the teaching and usages of St. Clement's Church.

On March 11, 1878, Prescott dashed off a brief note of thanks to the Reverend C. George Currie, who had intervened on behalf of Prescott and his priest associates in Cowley about the matter of their street dress.[154] On the street and in church, the Cowley fathers wore a simple black cassock fastened at the waist with a black cord cincture. Prescott and his associates thus attired were apparently unwelcome in certain places in Philadelphia and Dr. Currie had protested this discrimination. Controversy seemed to energize Prescott. On April 29, 1878, he wrote to three Philadelphia Episcopal clergymen about a reliable report which he had received that they said that the clergy of St. Clement's

Church were circulating books and asking questions of a girl which were of an impure and indelicate nature. He assures them that this is not true of any of the clergy at St. Clement's and asks that this rumor be denied. The letters were sent to the Reverend C. G. Currie, Rector of St. Luke's Church (to whom he had written a note of thanks just a few weeks previously), the Reverend E. A. Hoffman, Rector of St. Mark's Church (and later the Dean of General Theological Seminary in New York) and the Reverend R. Thomas. To Hoffman the report was that the clergy of St. Clement's were visiting among the people of St. Mark's and drawing them away from their church. On the same date, Prescott wrote the Reverend H. Stuart, who alleged that Prescott described to him questions which he would feel at liberty to ask "even nice women" coming to him for confession. On May 2, Prescott sent a second letter to Mr. Currie asking about the allegation that the clergy of St. Clement's have asked persons "indelicate or indecent questions." On May 4, a further letter goes to the clergymen who alleged that the clergy of St. Clement's were circulating "indecent books." This charge probably stemmed from a copy of an aid to confession or an examination of conscience guide.[155] Prescott was assertive in promptly tracking down and denying false rumors which were circulating about him and his clergy at St. Clement's and to defend their good character.

In the fall of 1877, St. Clement's had established the "Collegiate School of St. John." We do not know anything about the School, apart from its impressive name and the fact that the Reverend William R. Longridge S.S.J.E., one of the clergy on the staff of St. Clement's, was listed as its Headmaster. On May 8, 1878, Prescott wrote Bishop Stevens explaining that he had only recently learned that there was a canonical requirement that schools supported by the Church must report to the Bishop.[156] Prescott then asks Bishop Stevens to be the

Official Visitor of the School. In his reply, Bishop Stevens says that he must see the charter, constitution and rules of the School before he can agree to be its Official Visitor.[157]

In his reply to the Bishop, dated May 15, Prescott explains that the Collegiate School is not yet incorporated and, therefore, does not have a written charter and constitution.[158] Nevertheless, Prescott hopes that the Bishop will accept the position of Official Visitor with the assurance that when the constitution and rules are written, they will be submitted to him. This letter was written as the Bishop was about to leave for England to attend the Second Lambeth Conference of Anglican Bishops in London. Prescott opens his heart to the Bishop at length in the following words:

> I have never had so definite an idea of the very great difficulties of a position like yours, as I have just now. My whole heart has gone out to you in earnest sympathy during the last few days, and I beg you to believe that it is a great cross to me that I should seem to be obliged to add to yours. I am sorry that we cannot see eye to eye. As I look at things, if I were to yield to my feelings and act accordingly, I should cut away the very foundation on which I stand. Canonical obedience is the only obedience which I can offer you. If I were obliged to yield the passive obedience of a Romanist it would kill out all my faith in Christianity. I must stand where I do or I should abandon myself to float I do not know where.
>
> I have, I am told, a very abrupt manner and I easily excite antagonism and give offense. Will you kindly overlook

whatever there may have been of this in the past, and will you please believe me when I say that I do wish, from the very bottom of my heart that I could win your confidence and affection.

Prescott's letter was apparently hand-delivered to the Bishop because he replied that same day expressing sorrow for the "occasional differences of thought and action between us" and assuring Prescott that he gladly overlooks any hastiness of words and disrespect of manner on Prescott's part.[159]

Meanwhile, at the Diocesan Convention held earlier in May 1878, the ritual practices of St. Clement's were the subject of considerable discussion and debate. It was probably to this event that Prescott was alluding when he wrote to the Bishop expressing his "earnest sympathy during the last few days." The Convention adopted the following Resolution:[160]

> For a considerable time past rumors have been prevalent and wide-spread—rumors, it may be, too readily repeated and too easily magnified—that practices and usages and modes of worship inconsistent with the Constitution and Canons, the doctrines, discipline and worship of the Protestant Episcopal Church, and even utterly subversive of her Protestant character, have been allowed and sustained by the Vestry of St. Clement's Church, to the scandal of the community, the disturbance of the peace of this Church, and the great pain and grief of her people, <u>Therefore Resolved</u>, That a Committee of Inquiry, consisting of clergymen and laymen, be appointed to ascertain the facts and recommend

such action, if any, as they may deem expedient in the premises, and to report either to this or to the next Annual Convention.

It is noteworthy that the Resolution makes no mention of National Canon 22 adopted in 1874 dealing with ritual controversies and that the Resolution names the Vestry, but not the clergy of St. Clement's as responsible for the ritual practices of that Parish.

On July 31, Prescott wrote to three of his clergy neighbors, Dr. Currie, Mr. Stuart and another whose name is illegible in the surviving copy.[161] In this letter Prescott explained that since he had been in Philadelphia, the clergy of St. Clement's "have found themselves drawn into a good deal of work among the poorest class of colored people" who live at such distances from the Church that it is impossible for them to attend services there. He proposes to open a chapel for the "exclusive use" of these people and, in accord with a canon passed at the last Diocesan Convention, he asked for formal permission of these clergy to open such a chapel in a neighborhood near their churches. Only Dr. Currie's reply has survived in which he states that the clergy of his parish, St. Luke's, have spent considerable time and money last spring working among "colored people" which they intend to resume, if possible, this fall.[162] Inasmuch as two missions in the same neighborhood are not advisable, Dr. Currie prefers to leave the matter to Prescott's Christian courtesy, rather than refusing "official consent." Prescott replies that St. Clement's more than a year ago rented a hall in the neighborhood of St. Luke's Church and now, as required by the new canon, is seeking only formal consent from Dr. Currie to continue that work there.[163] Reading between the lines, it would seem that the recent Diocesan canon was adopted for the express purpose of preventing St. Clement's from establishing any further missions or continuing this existing one. Prescott counters that St. Clement's is not now beginning to work among "colored people", but simply carrying it on.[164] It is a work which came to St. Clement's unsought and by God's Providence and he feels it would be wrong to lay it down now. The final word from Dr. Currie was a polite refusal to give formal and official consent to the mission.[165] We don't know whether the mission to poor African-Americans continued under St. Clement's or others.

On November 9, 1878, Prescott again wrote the Bishop to inform him that several persons in the Parish were preparing for confirmation and expressing the hope that the Bishop could schedule a visit to St. Clement's some weekday at 4 p.m. during the first half of next Lent.[166] Needless to say, the request was not granted and no visit for confirmation was scheduled by Bishop Stevens.

In an undated letter to a layman named James Hammond, Prescott seeks to counter the rumor that St. Clement's is supported by money from England and elsewhere.[167] Prescott explains that the parish is able to do all it does chiefly because of the devoted support of its parishioners and because the clergy live under the vow of poverty, taking only what they need for the necessities of life.

From February 2 to 14, 1879, Father Grafton and the Reverend W. J. King-Little conducted a mission at St. Clement's Church. King-Little was Canon Residentiary of Worcester Cathedral in England and a leading ritualist. The mission is described in detail in the Report of the Committee of Inquiry into St. Clement's Church mandated by action of the 1878 Diocesan Convention.[168] Each of the twelve days of the mission included a Bible class in the chapel at noon conducted by Fr. Grafton with about 75 persons present. The evening services began at 7:30 p.m. and were held in the Church, which was filled or very nearly filled, each night. Grafton preached the first nights and Canon King-Little preached from Friday evening to the conclusion of the mission. The reporter described the congregation in the evenings as very attentive and found Canon King-Little's sermons very earnest and impressive. As might be expected, the theological content was from an Anglo-Catholic perspective.

In April 1879, Prescott had an exchange of letters with the now aged Bishop Whittingham which must have been extremely painful to Prescott.[169] Prescott had been invited to preach at Mt. Calvary Church in Baltimore. But, in conformity with the Bishop's request, the invitation had been withdrawn. Prescott replies that he will, of course, respect the Bishop's wishes. But Prescott wonders further whether he may continue ministering to the All Saints Sisters at their convent in the Diocese of Maryland. He promises to do this as quietly as possible and to confine his work to the Sisters' house, if the Bishop wishes. Bishop Whittingham's reply was written by his daughter, Margaret H. Whittingham, because the Bishop was now physically unable to write. He expressed "the kindliest personal regards for Prescott" but he was unable in any way to sanction Prescott's ministrations in his Diocese because he is a member of the Cowley Brotherhood. While the Bishop was an old fashioned high Churchman, he was opposed to the reintroduction of the monastic system. He opposed the All Saints sisters as well as the Cowley fathers. It is not clear why and how the former were tolerated in his Diocese while the latter were forbidden. In his answer, Prescott explains that he was opposed to the All Saints sisters going to Maryland, but only loyalty to Bishop Whittingham and to Mr. Richey, the late Rector of Mt. Calvary Church, prevented him from urging the sisters to leave Maryland. Apparently, at that time

Prescott was unaware of Bishop Whittingham's opposition to religious communities. At any rate, there the sisters have stayed and continue to this day. Finally, Prescott begs permission to visit one of the All Saints sisters who is terminally ill. Prescott concludes that the Bishop's "least wish shall be law to me."

Following the action of the 1878 Pennsylvania Diocesan Convention authorizing an inquiry into St. Clement's Church, a spate of pamphlets was published by both high and low Churchmen in that Diocese. The first appears to have been by the Secretary of the Evangelical Educational Society, the Reverend Robert C. Matlack, who published his address to the Convention entitled, "Our Great Danger and Our Great Responsibility."[170] This was promptly answered in June 1878 by a pamphlet written by Mr. George W. Hunter, defending Catholic principles and entitled, "The Holy Eucharist and Auricular Confession."[171] In March 1879, Hunter expanded the first edition of this pamphlet from 42 to 60 pages and added an appendix of 85 pages citing many ecclesiastical authorities in support of his position—a total of 145 pages![172] Mr. Hunter's pamphlet roused the Reverend Dr. C. George Currie to take up his pen and write a pamphlet on "Ritualism as Defended by Mr. Hunter."[173] Whereupon Henry Flanders, a lawyer and Warden of St. Clement's Church, wrote a reply to Dr. Currie entitled, "Pennsylvania Protestant Episcopalianism Not the Religion of the Bible and Prayer Book."[174] Meanwhile, the Reverend Dr. Daniel R. Goodwin had authored a pamphlet. Dr. Goodwin was the President of the Standing Committee of the Diocese of Pennsylvania, one of its Deputies to the General Convention, the Dean of the Philadelphia Divinity School and the mover of the resolution at the 1878 Convention to investigate St. Clement's Church. He was a most distinguished priest of the Diocese and the apparent leader of the Evangelical party there. On February 5,

1879, Prescott addressed a nine page open letter to Dr. Goodwin which was published under the title, "Is Fairness in Religious Controversy Impossible?"[175] In this letter, Prescott urges the parties to listen to and try to learn from each other, rather than trying to annihilate each other. On February 14 Dr. Goodwin promptly published his "Presbyter's Reply to the Priest's Letter." By this time the 1,000 copies of Prescott's letter had all sold and he added a postscript and had it reprinted. Sometime in 1879, several members of the May 1878 Convention published a pamphlet raising serious questions about the parliamentary procedures followed when the Convention adopted the resolution to investigate St. Clement's Church. This publication was entitled, "What It Meant and How It Was Done."[176] Its authors did not support St. Clement's but they questioned the way in which the resolution was put through the Convention in 1878. In the midst of all this heavy pamphleteering, someone wrote and printed a comic, satirical pamphlet on the whole business entitled, "The Report of the Committee Appointed to Investigate Mr. John Jones and His Family."[177]

On May 3, 1879, Prescott wrote Dr. Goodwin thanking him for correcting an error which Prescott made in his pamphlet.[178] This correction was made by Dr. Goodwin in the second edition of his pamphlet. Prescott closes his letter by "protesting against (Goodwin's) circulation of so unfair and misleading a publication."

At the Annual Diocesan Convention of Pennsylvania on May 6, 1879, the Committee of Inquiry into St. Clement's Church made its report.[179] The Committee consisted of three clergy, including the Reverend Dr. Goodwin, and three laymen. The supporting documents included in the Committee's report included accounts of visits to four services at St. Clement's, including Whitsunday and Christmas, 1878. The services were all choral Eucharist at which the celebrant alone received the consecrated elements. The observers note a choir of fifty members with cornet and trumpet in the procession as well as drummer and bass viol. At Christmas, there was a "profusion of flowers" and at all four services forty or more candles burned on and around the altar. Eucharistic vestments were worn. One observer noted that: "The services were imposing; much finer than any I ever saw in Romish Churches abroad."

Another observer reported that at a Sunday evening service in February 1879, "the Church was filled. The majority of the congregation were young people; young men especially. The greatest attention was paid to the instructions."

On May 22, 1879 Prescott writes Bishop Stevens that at the request of the Vestry of St. Timothy's Parish he has become its Acting Rector for one year.[180] Prescott asks the Bishop to appoint a visitation to St. Timothy's some week night during Whitsun week. There are probably fifty or sixty persons ready and desirous of being confirmed whom Prescott would like to present to the Bishop. Prescott apologizes for suggesting the time of the Bishop's appointment, but explains that his passage to Europe is booked for Thursday after Trinity Sunday. We may assume that many of those fifty or sixty persons were members of St. Clement's Church. The Bishop declines the invitation and says that the proceedings of the Easter election at St. Timothy's were so "irregular, if not absolutely illegal" that he is not prepared to acknowledge their validity or to recognize Prescott as Acting Rector of that Parish.[181] In spite of Prescott's repeatedly expressed wish to be the Bishop's filial and obedient priest, Prescott's actions further alienated and upset Bishop Stevens.

The Bishop wrote Prescott on June 2 that he and the Standing Committee had set June 9, 1879 for the examination called for in the recent Convention's Resolution, in accordance with Canon 22 of the National Church.[182] Prescott replied the same day asking that the investigation be postponed because he must be out of the city for seven weeks.[183] This presumably was to attend the Annual Retreat of his Community at Cowley in England. This was followed the next day by a letter from Prescott to Bishop Stevens inquiring if he would be permitted legal advisers and a secretary to accompany him at the investigation.[184] The requests were apparently granted because in the published text of the investigation, the proceedings begin on Tuesday, January 20, 1880.[185]

There is an interesting partial copy of a letter which Prescott wrote on September 6, 1879 addressed only to "My dear Rev. Brother."[186] In it Prescott writes, "I take very great interest in your people." This must refer to African-Americans because in the next sentence Prescott adds:

> The Bishop of Haiti is an old and valued friend and I think that the American Episcopal (Church) is very greatly honored in having him among its members. There are few among his brethren who are his equal and I don't know of but one (Bishop Whittingham) who is his superior. For his sake, and for your sake, I will do what I can to forward your work.

The Bishop of Haiti, here mentioned only by title, was James Theodore Holly, who was born in 1829. A self-educated man of color, he was ordained a deacon in 1855 and a priest early in 1856. He served as Rector of St. Luke's Church, New Haven, from 1855 to 1865, when he led a group of his parishioners to colonize a place in Haiti. They suffered great hardship there. But Holly survived and in 1874 was ordained the first Episcopal Bishop of Haiti in which office he served until his death in 1911. Prescott had ample opportunity to become acquainted with Bishop Holly during visits to New Haven from 1855 onwards when Holly was serving St. Luke's Church there.

The proceedings of this new investigation were published (probably by St. Clement's Church) under the title, "The Trial of the Rev. O.S. Prescott Before the Standing Committee of the Diocese of Pennsylvania."[187] The document runs to 133 pages. The trial opens with the Standing Committee calling for and hearing testimony from several witnesses on the evenings of January 20 and 27. The questions and answers in this interrogation are printed verbatim and deal chiefly with the ritual practices in choral celebrations of the Holy Communion at St. Clement's Church. Mr. George W. Biddle is counsel for the defense. The ceremonies were the same as those described in the Report of the Committee of Inquiry to the Diocesan Convention the previous May.

On February 3, Prescott addressed a statement to Bishop Stevens clarifying the ceremonial usage at St. Clement's pertaining to the seven charges in his presentment, viz.: 1) genuflections, bowing and prostrations; 2) use of candles; 3) clerical vestments; 4) elevation of the bread and wine during or after the consecration; 5) use of acolytes; 6) non-communicating celebrations of the Holy Communion; and 7) the use of unauthorized prayers, hymns, sentences and rites. Prescott denies certain false or mistaken allegations. The accuracy of this statement is attested by the three assisting clergy at St. Clement's, the Reverend B.W. Maturin, the Reverend D. Convers, and the Reverend Wilberforce Wells. In this statement Prescott notes that the vestments worn by the clergy at the altar in St. Clement's are those he found in use when he became the rector and "such as he has worn ever since he was made a priest in 1848."

At the February 16 session, further witnesses were called and examined. When Fr. Prescott was called to testify, represented by his counsel, George W. Biddle, Prescott declined to appear. He did so believing that it was contrary to all regular procedure that the body which could (if he was found offending) admonish him, was also to cross-examine him. In other words, Prescott objected that the Bishop and Standing Committee were both also his prosecutors and judge.

At the February 16 session, three of the lawyers representing Prescott and the Parish testified on his behalf. Biddle made it clear that Canon 22 was really on trial, not Prescott. The counsel asserted that the Church adopts rubrics not by canons, but by changes in its Prayer Book. Further, the canon was vague in its term "doubtful doctrines." Biddle then argued that six of the seven charges against Prescott must be thrown out because they are not covered in Canon 22. Only the matter of bowings and genuflections and prostrations are covered in Canon 22. Here Biddle maintains that the kneeling by clergy and others during the Communion is not in violation of the Prayer Book rubrics. His lengthy statement is a very clear and forceful defense of Prescott.

Mr. Henry Flanders, who was also an attorney as well as Warden at St. Clement's Church, further advances these arguments. He defends St. Clement's as:

> A congregation of a thousand souls . . . as devout and as energetic in all that concerns the common faith as any other in this diocese or in this land, a congregation . . . which, in an age of unbelief, has apparently believed more fully and reverently than others, has been continually hawked at, and publicly assailed whenever a public opportunity has offered.

Flanders concluded that "By opposing the inevitable, we create unavailing strife, distract the church, and subvert its dignity and its influence."

Finally, Mr. William S. Price presented his statement on behalf of Fr. Prescott and St. Clement's Church. His was the concluding statement of the defense.

On April 14, 1880, the Standing Committee of the Diocese reported to the Bishop that it found that Prescott had indeed introduced the seven practices at St. Clement's Church with which he was charged. Thereupon Bishop Stevens once again admonished Prescott to discontinue these practices and ceremonies—only this time the Bishop was acting under national Canon 22. The Bishop concluded with a strange denial.

> This, as you well know, has not been a trial, either of you or of your church (emphasis the Bishop's). It has been simply an investigation by a competent and lawful authority as to whether certain alleged rites and ceremonies have, or have not been, introduced into, and are in use in your church.
>
> Nor is this admonition of mine punitive (emphasis the Bishop's).

One wonders why another investigation was needed when the Committee of Inquiry eleven months before had reported that the alleged usages were found in St. Clement's Church. And what further force would the Bishop's second admonition have which his first one lacked?

Six days later, Prescott having had opportunity to confer with his counsel sent a long reply to the Bishop's admonition. Prescott reminds the Bishop that on January 22, 1873 he (the Bishop) wrote the Reverend

Theodore M. Riley, who was then the Rector of St. Clement's, in relation to the same ceremonies and practices which he now accuses Prescott of introducing into the parish. Prescott has simply conformed to what he found at St. Clement's when he became its rector. Prescott respectfully differs with the Bishop that what has just transpired is not a trial of St. Clement's and that the admonition is not punitive. Prescott then proceeds to reply once again to the various charges and to the dubious legality of Canon 22 under the Constitution of the Episcopal Church.

Two days later Bishop Stevens writes Prescott:

> I deeply regret that you should so far forget yourself as to bring a railing accusation against those set in authority over you, as you have so offensively done in your letter.

Then, on April 24, Prescott replies that he is neither submitting nor declining to submit to the Bishop's requests. Because of the many interests involved, he will need time to consider his response to the Bishop's admonition.

On May 5, 1880, Prescott submits his resignation to the Vestry of St. Clement's. He does so because, he writes:

> I cannot use my office as your minister or your priest to wrest from you your rights as a congregation at the dictation of those who have ignored my rights as a rector in asking me to ignore your rights as a parish. I cannot so shirk my moral responsibility, and I therefore lay before you my resignation of my rectorship.

He concludes by expressing his gratitude for their affection and their steadfast support in the midst of trouble.

But the Vestry, two days later, earnestly requests Prescott to withdraw his resignation. If he does, they are prepared to advise him to acquiesce in the Bishop's demands. "They prefer to give up some of the accessories of worship rather than lose their rector." The Vestry feels this will best serve the interests of the Parish.

Accordingly, on May 8 Prescott wrote the Bishop that "in conformity to the request of his vestry" . . . he shall abstain from the practices and ceremonies referred to in the finding of the Standing Committee. The Bishop replied on May 8 accepting this statement with much satisfaction and regarding it as a "true and explicit submission to the lawful authority of this Diocese."[188] The Bishop also agreed to visit St. Clement's on Friday, May 28 for the rite of confirmation. Prescott had written that there were some sixty to seventy-five persons under his spiritual care who were ready and desirous of being confirmed.

With Prescott's agreement to abstain from the practices and usages to which the Bishop so strenuously objected, his long trial ended. For the next eighteen months the conduct of worship at St. Clement's conformed to Bishop Steven's requirements. Prescott's was the first trial for ritual offenses under Canon 22. A church historian has written that as far as he can discover, Prescott is the only clergyman in the Episcopal Church to be tried under this canon.[189] The canon was poorly written with its mention of "doubtful doctrines." It was also unenforceable. In 1904, without a single voice being raised in its defense, the General Convention repealed the canon intended to enforce ritual uniformity. In 1867, when the ritual controversy was growing, the Rt. Rev. John Henry Hopkins, the Bishop of Vermont, observed, "Ritualism will grow into favor by degrees until it becomes the prevailing system."[190] In 1979,

105 years after the "Ritual" canon was adopted, the Episcopal Church adopted a new revision of the <u>Book of Common Prayer</u> incorporating or allowing virtually every ritual practice which the canon sought to forbid!

Members or possibly friends, of St. Clement's Church, had issued two pamphlets with details of the Trial. One was the lengthy account already referred to which included verbatim accounts of interrogations and statements by the three lawyers in defense of the Parish. A briefer account was also published under the title, "The Charges Against the Rector of St. Clement's Church . . . Together with his Statements, Explanations, Protest and Arguments of Counsel."[191] Apparently, in consequence of these two publications supportive of St. Clement's, the Reverend Dr. Daniel R. Goodwin was moved to publish, on May 7, 1880, his "Notes of the Investigation by the Bishop and Standing Committee in Reference to Certain Practices at St. Clement's Church."[192] The pamphlet was 42 pages long including a 15 page Abstract of the Testimony at the Trial. This appears to be the last of the pamphlets which the Trial prompted.

Prescott, ever quick to be on the defensive, took exception to some statements in the Abstract of Testimony by Mr. Harold Goodwin, Esq., printed in the Reverend Daniel Goodwin's "Notes, etc.,". On June 12, 1880 then, Prescott wrote Mr. Harold Goodwin challenging his account of a week-day celebration at St. Clement's on Corpus Christi Day at which Prescott was the celebrant."[193] Prescott proposes to set against Mr. Goodwin's testimony the affidavits of several of the persons who were present at that service to substantiate his refutation. Prescott concludes that this correspondence is, of course, for publication. Mr. Goodwin replied on June 15, though we do not have a copy of his letter.

However, the following day Prescott carefully drafted a six page plea to Mr. Goodwin refuting his testimony that prayers other than from the <u>Book of Common Prayer</u> had been used at St. Clement's and reminding Mr. Goodwin of Prescott's written statement to that effect which was endorsed by the three assisting clergy at St. Clement's.[194] Prescott's concern is for the truth which he feels was not well served at his trial.

There is a partial copy of a letter which Prescott wrote on October 18, 1880 from New York addressed to "Rev. Mother" regarding work of Sisters in Philadelphia.[195] In this letter, Prescott speaks of the house which they opened in Philadelphia a year ago and of the current need for more nursing sisters there. Prescott then mentions several sisters by name and discusses their needs and concerns. There is also extant a letter from the Rev. Mother Superior of All Saints addressed to "Rev. Father."[196] This letter, dated only November 6, speaks of a group of sisters who will be leaving Liverpool on November 11 to come to the United States. It is likely that these were the sisters who then came to Philadelphia under St. Clement's auspices and to whom Prescott refers in his draft letter of October 18, 1880.

From November 8 to 13, 1880 Canon King-Little gave a retreat for priests at St. Clement's Church. Two of the priests attending the retreat were Robert Dod and James Huntington.[197] Both were young and both had been ordained priest within the year. The retreat had a powerful effect on both men. Huntington wrote to his brother on November 23:

> I wish you could have been with me at the Retreat. It was wonderfully helpful. I do not care to think what might have become of me without it. It seems to me not too much to say that it was God's provision for saving my soul.[198]

Dod had been working at the Holy Cross Mission on the lower east side of New York City where he had frequent contact with the St. John the Baptist Sisters. Shortly after the retreat, Dod went to England and was received as a postulant at Cowley on February 4, 1881. Huntington returned to Calvary Church and St. Mark's Church in Syracuse, N.Y., where he had been working. This is the first of several convergences between Prescott and Fr. Huntington and Fr. Dod who were two of the founding members of the Order of the Holy Cross in the United States. In 1881, Prescott's sister, Emily (known in the convent as Sister Augustine) was a member of the Community of St. John the Baptist in New York.

A brief note survives which Prescott wrote to a parishioner, Mrs. Diehl, to clarify a misunderstanding over her daughter's wedding.[199] It reveals his concern and care to restore a right relationship between himself and this parishioner.

In February 1881, Prescott received another blow.[200] In 1879, William Pinckney succeeded William Whittingham as Bishop of Maryland. On February 4, 1881, Bishop Pinckney sent a one sentence letter to Prescott informing him that he was "inhibited from the exercise of any and every function of (his) holy office in the Diocese of Maryland." Prescott replied from New York on February 8 that he would accept this in silence if he understood it. He asks whether the Bishop's action is in consequence of something that Prescott had done in the past or because of something which he might do in the future. To this inquiry, Prescott received no reply from Bishop Pinckney. Accordingly, Prescott wrote Bishop Pinckney on February 15 and again on February 21 asking that receipt of his letter be acknowledged by the Bishop. Finally, on February 21, Pinckney replied declining to enter into a discussion of the reasons for his action.

This understandably upset Prescott who discussed the matter with his own Bishop. Bishop Stevens indicated to Prescott that he thought an explanation was due him from Bishop Pinckney. Prescott accordingly wrote Bishop Pinckney saying that he wished he knew of a way that he could vindicate the rights of his priestly order without seeming rude. But he does not know of such a way. Therefore, he is obliged to send back to Bishop Pinckney the so-called "inhibition." He cannot retain it without an explanation. If it is returned to him by Bishop Pinckney without explanation, Prescott will not regard it as of any force or account whatsoever.

Fr. Benson traveled to the United States twice in 1880, at the beginning and at the end of the year. On both occasions he tried to resolve the tensions at St. Clement's.[201] He wrote that:

> Some things . . . would have been different if I had had control of the parochial management. I certainly should have urged more hearty acceptance of episcopal authority.

Fr. Benson asked Prescott to resign as Rector of St. Clement's. According to a lengthy letter which Prescott wrote to the Wardens and Vestry of St. Clement's on November 17, 1881, Fr. Benson did not make this a matter of obedience, but only one of three courses any one of which he would approve.[202] However, Fr. Benson did state that if Prescott chose to continue as Rector of St. Clement's, he (Benson, that is) would withdraw all the other members of the Society from the Parish. In the spring of 1881, Prescott requested, and was granted by the Vestry, a leave of absence. He was gone from the Parish for five months, from June 23 to November 23. Prescott left Fr. Maturin in charge of St. Clement's. If Prescott returned as Rector on November 23, on that date the assisting priests would be withdrawn by the Society.

We do not know what the three acceptable courses were which Fr. Benson presented to Prescott. Fr. Benson was too astute to suggest that Prescott return to St. Clement's as an assistant under Fr. Maturin as rector. That would not only put Maturin in an impossibly difficult position, it would also quickly polarize the parish. Nor is it likely that Benson suggested that Prescott return to St. Clement's and serve there alone without the other members of the Society. Fr. Benson was in communication with the other members of the Society at St. Clement's and probably knew that if they all left, so would many members of the parish. This would leave the parish greatly weakened and facing possible bankruptcy which might eventually lead to the demise of the parish. Further, if Prescott returned alone to St. Clement's, he would be faced with conducting the services without the usual ceremonies which meant much to him and the parishioners. Any way he looked at it, returning to St. Clement's was not a viable option for Prescott. If he resigned, then where would he go? Fr. Benson may have suggested that he be assigned to Boston.

Since March 1877, there had been two centers of the Society's ministry in Boston: the Church of the Advent, now located in a new building on Brimmer Street, was the headquarters of the work, and the old building, on Bowdoin Street (which the Society had purchased), was a mission subject to the rector of the Advent but independent of that parish.[203] If Prescott were to go to Boston, he would be an assistant to Fr. Grafton. While the two priests were old friends, would a proud man like Prescott be willing to accept this? Finally, Fr. Benson may have suggested that Prescott resign as Rector of St. Clement's and return to Cowley in England and do mission work there. Prescott had much experience in conducting missions and conducted them well. But this would put Prescott in close proximity to Fr. Benson and that option may not have appealed to Prescott.

Part of Prescott's problem involved reconciling his obligations as a priest of the American Episcopal Church with his obligations as a member of a foreign society (that is, the S. S. J. E.). As an American Rector, Prescott felt bound to make the Parish his first interest, while Fr. Benson thought that the Society should have been Prescott's first consideration.[204] This tension was enhanced by the fact that Fr. Benson, as a priest of the Church of England, "had little or no knowledge of our national churches—the Constitution and Canons of our Church and the practical working of our ecclesiastical system."[205]

On July 28, Prescott wrote Fr. Benson from Prescott's sister's home in New Haven. In this letter Prescott cited two instances in which he felt this tension acutely. During one of Benson's visits to Philadelphia the previous year, without a word to Prescott, Fr. Benson put a stop to the nursing ministry of the All Saints Sisters which they had undertaken at Prescott's invitation. Benson's only answer was that "nursing the sick was not proper work for Sisters of the Poor."[206] Also last year, after Prescott had promised to respect Bishop Whittingham's request to abstain from ministering in the Diocese of Maryland, Benson directed one of Prescott's assistants, without consulting Prescott, to be Chaplain to the Sisters in Baltimore.

Father Grafton, who was at this time the Rector of the Church of the Advent in Boston, had similar concerns. The Society of St. John the Evangelist had a spiritual rule of life but no written constitution. Grafton believed that the Society, in order to have the moral support of Bishops in America, must have a written constitution to submit to them for their approval.[207] There was further the need for some separation of the work of the Society in America from its work in England, a goal which was not to be realized for many years.

Mr. Henry Flanders, the Warden of St. Clement's, wrote Prescott on September 21 and said:

> Candor compels me to say that your return, accompanied as it would be, by the withdrawal of the other members of the Society, would be the virtual disruption and dissolution of the Parish.[208]

Flanders begs Prescott "to avoid the position of antagonism with your Society and preserve intact your connection with it." Prescott replies to Mr. Flanders on October 16:

> If the Vestrymen of St. Clement's think that the time has come when a dissolution of our connection is desirable, it is open to them to say so, giving their reasons with frankness and freedom and submitting the matter to my consideration.[209]

On October 17, a Vestryman, Mr. R.L. Wright, wrote Prescott that he believes that if Fr. Maturin leaves, one-third of the people will go, and those the most liberal contributors.

Sometime during this period, Prescott chose to consult Bishop Stevens about what he should do. It seemed a strange thing to do because they had been adversaries for so long. We do not know what the Bishop advised Prescott. At the end of October a group of twenty-seven members of St. Clement's signed a long statement addressed to Prescott. They found Prescott's desire for the Bishop's counsel or intervention:

> As incomprehensible to the members of this parish as the
> step itself is repugnant to their judgment and wishes . . .
> Your people are unable to see in what manner, or upon what
> subjects, any intervention of the Bishop can be deemed at
> this crisis either needful or tolerable, at least to them.[210]

The signers repeat the fear that if the Society withdraws the assistants on Prescott's return, many parishioners will also withdraw and parish finances will fall drastically. The signers identify themselves as Prescott's warm personal friends.

Finally, on November 18, Prescott submitted his resignation to the Vestry.[211] He wrote that rather than keep up a struggle he "preferred to be driven" from his Rectorship. His resignation took effect on November 23 when his leave of absence expired. Leaving St. Clement's must have been one of the most painful moments in Prescott's life. He had faced crises before which had led to his resigning as Rector. Twice he had precipitated the crisis—at Ellicott's Mills and at Trinity Church, Newport. But Prescott and his colleagues in the Society had been at St. Clement's five and one-half years during which the parish had grown greatly. He had many friends and loyal supporters there whom it would be difficult to leave. At the same time, it might have been some relief to be able to leave Bishop Stevens' jurisdiction and once again to celebrate the Eucharist with full ceremonial.

Following Prescott's resignation, Fr. Maturin became the Rector of St. Clement's. He had come to the parish in February 1876 with Prescott and knew the parish well. Like Prescott, he was a good preacher. Fr. Maturin soon restored the old ceremonial and introduced the use of incense, the ne plus ultra of ritualism to Evangelical Episcopalians.[212] He doubtless succeeded in thus restoring and further "advancing" the ceremonial because the existing agreement was between Prescott and Bishop Stevens. Maturin, as a priest of the Church of England, was not subject to Bishop Stevens' jurisdiction. Also, the Bishop may have grown weary of trying to stamp out ritualism in his Diocese. Forty years later, a subsequent rector of St. Clement's looked back on the years under Fr. Maturin as St. Clement's time of greatest glory with crowds coming to hear him preach. The Cowley fathers continued serving at St. Clement's until 1891.

Oliver Sherman Prescott

Father Oliver Sherman Prescott

Father Oliver S. Prescott, SSJE
Rector of St. Clements Church
Philadelphia, Penn.
1876-1881"

WISCONSIN: THE DIOCESE OF FOND DU LAC

Just three months after his resignation, Prescott learned of the death of his younger brother, William, in New Haven at the age of 52.[213] Because he was in Milwaukee at the time, Prescott was unable to attend his brother's funeral. During the five months of his leave from St. Clement's, Fr. Prescott visited in his brother's home where his sister, Mary, also lived.

On January 10, 1882, writing from Westboro, Mass., Prescott replied to a letter from a Mr. Brand (or Brauer, the handwriting is not clear), in which Prescott said that he felt not much, if any, sense of personal mortification over his leaving St. Clement's, but rather, "profound perplexity and bewilderment."[214] Prescott denies the rumor that if he had returned to St. Clement's it would have been as a secular priest. Prescott then asserts that there was no talk among the American members of the S.S.J.E. of forming an American branch of the Society because from the beginning he and Fr. Grafton <u>were</u> the American branch (as Fr. Benson and Fr. O'Neill were the English branch). The English priests of the S.S.J.E. are not, and cannot be, part of the American branch without becoming naturalized citizens here. The question which <u>has</u> come up is whether the time has come for the American branch to take up a more open existence. On this "question the Americans are on one side and Fr. Benson on the other . . . It seems quite impossible for Fr. Benson to understand the position of our Bishops." Benson feels that:

> The less they (i.e. bishops) have to do with us and we with them the better. This may be true in England but we do not think that it is true here. We feel that it is impossible for our Society to be what it ought to be if the Episcopate is united

against it and wc know that to a man our Bishops are against it, as it is presented to them with a foreign ecclesiastic as its head and its parishes held as missions from Cowley, and we know that many Bishops would be with us, if it were presented to them as it really is.

Prescott wrote Fr. Benson from Milwaukee on February 16, 1882 about the need for a conference to workout differences in the S.S.J.E.[215] Prescott said:

> Leaving out all consideration of personal grievance because of the way in which I have been treated by you, I feel that as a member of the Society of St. John I ought to tell you that unless something is done to settle the difficulties in the Boston and Philadelphia houses and in the relations of these houses to each other, we shall find ourselves in a scandal as low and as disastrous as our own aims have been high and happy.

> I see only one way out of this trouble and that is by you asking Fr. O'Neill home from India and Fr. Grafton and myself out to Cowley to consider and arrange the whole matter of the relationship of the English portion of the Society to the American branch and so clear the way for a constitution which shall recognize the fact that the Society is a coalition of priests belonging to two separate and independent Churches. Surely we, whose coming together made the discipline of the Society possible, can, after the wide experience and deep trouble which we have had, do something towards its organization and perpetration. Believe me, dear Fr. Benson, something must be done and that soon.

It was not until 1914 that an autonomous American Congregation of the S.S.J.E. was to become a reality.[216] One year later, Fr. Benson died. Not until 1920 did the American province of the Society become fully independent of the English province.

On May 22, Prescott, in Philadelphia, wrote to Fr. Benson enclosing a letter from Fr. Walter R. Gardner S. S. J. E.[217] Prescott told Benson that "humanly speaking no one but you can be of any help in this matter." In the enclosed letter which Fr. Gardner wrote to Prescott from Boston, Gardner said:

> I have a great deal I want to say to you. I shall be so glad to get away from here. This way of living is terrible to me. Such an utter disappointment as regards my whole life and those I have looked up to. It seems sometimes as though I would go mad and I believe I should go mad if I had not made up my mind that I won't. Do find and suggest some way for giving me a very early respite.[218]

Prescott writes Fr. Benson again on July 4, this time from Milwaukee, saying:[219]

> No matter where the fault may lay the remedy lies with you only. You must . . . acknowledge that there is a possibility that you and others who go along with you may be mistaken in ascribing the difficulties to mere personal grievance or personal ambition.

Prescott then adds:

> When I was turned penniless into the street to live as I could,
> I went as a matter of course to the only house of the Society
> that was open to me and so the house in Boston is my
> home . . . I cannot consent to leave America at present unless
> it is for a limited time and for the purpose of attending a
> Chapter or conference called to settle existing difficulties . . .
> I cannot be reconciled to (the brethren in Philadelphia) for I
> have not fallen out with them. I have only pleasant relations
> with Fr. Maturin.

Evidently, Fr. Benson was urging Prescott to return to Cowley in England permanently which Prescott was reluctant to do except to take part in Chapter Meeting to discuss the relationship of the English and American clergy in the Society. Finally, on August 14, Fr. Benson released Prescott and Grafton and Walter Gardner from their life vows.

Prescott responds with deep gratitude on August 16 from Milwaukee, "I thank you with a full heart, as one who needed it, for the release you have given us from all claims of obedience to yourself as the Head of the Cowley House."[220] Prescott goes on to explain:

> I do not in any way consider myself released from my
> obligation as one of the priests of the American branch of this
> Society of St. John the Evangelist which I joined, or thought
> myself to be joining and all that as an American priest.

Prescott says that before long he hopes all the American members of the Society can meet in Conference. He believes there are only four—the three just released that month and Fr. Edward Benedict. Prescott claims that "The reality of constitutional government in this country fosters a constitutional mind . . . in our citizens." When Prescott writes that "in the American Church the Bishops may have little power" as contrasted to English Bishops, he must be referring to civil power and authority because English Bishops are officers of the State. At the same time the American bishops' "influence is so great that it is suicidal to ignore it. If any religious work is to be done here it must be done along with the Bishops."

Sometime in 1882, probably soon after Prescott's resignation, Grafton wrote him a very solicitous personal letter in which he said:

> When you get to New Haven, don't read . . . Take a good deal of quiet outdoor exercise. Get a walk and go to bed very early, and get some fresh air just before going to bed at 8:30. At first you won't sleep, but I think you will by and by. Get to bed early and lie in bed. When you begin to worry, whistle a little. It makes one laugh, and laughing is a Divine Institution, sadly neglected in Religion.[221]

By 1883, Prescott was settled as Rector of St. Peter's Church in Ripon, Wisconsin in the Diocese of Fond du Lac. That same year he was elected a Clerical Deputy from the Fond du Lac Diocese to the General Convention of the Episcopal Church which met in Philadelphia October 3-26, 1883. The Diocese of Fond du Lac was young, having been separated in 1874 from the Diocese of Wisconsin (which thereupon became the Diocese of Milwaukee). The Diocesan territory was huge by Eastern standards, covering more than half of the state and 27,000 square miles. It had very little money, many mission churches needing financial subsidies, only nine self-supporting parishes and 18 active clergymen.[222] Its chief attraction for Prescott was that its Bishop, John Henry Hobart Brown, was an Anglo-Catholic and welcomed ritualist clergy like Prescott.

A private publication, probably printed by Fr. Gardner, contains the text of two letters which he wrote to Fr. Benson in 1883.[223] The first and longest, running to ten printed pages was written from Boston on March 15, 1883. The second, consisting of only a single page of printed text, was also written from Boston by Gardner to Benson on October 10, 1883. In his preface to this little publication, Fr. Gardner states that when the number of professed members of the S.S.J.E. increased to four (which was in 1870 when Prescott took life vows at Cowley), the three (O'Neill, Grafton and Prescott) agreed with Benson (whom they had elected the Superior) that when the number of professed fathers should reach twelve, a chapter would be convened for the purpose of drawing up a written constitution for the Society. In spite of this verbal agreement and the pressing need for it from those members working in American parishes, Fr. Benson refused to give any written constitution. Fr. Gardner also makes it clear that when the Church of the Advent began erecting its new building on Brimmer Street in Boston in order for Grafton to be in sole charge of that parish, he practically had to buy the resignation of the English priests in the Society by making it possible for the Society to purchase the Parish's old building on Bowdoin Street. From his family, Grafton contributed $10,000 to the Society which was a major gift toward its purchase of the Church on Bowdoin Street for a total of $27,000. The S.S.J.E. then took possession of the Bowdoin Street building which it ran as a private chapel, thereby putting it beyond the control of the Bishop of Massachusetts. The English priests of the Society were based on Bowdoin Street, which became known as the Church of St. John the Evangelist and Grafton was in sole charge of the Church of the Advent on Brimmer Street.

Gardner also states that in the summer of 1881, when Benson had told Prescott that if Prescott did not resign as Rector of St. Clement's he (Benson) would withdraw from the parish all the other members of the Society, Benson used the same tactic to force Grafton to accept Fr. Osborne as his assistant in Boston. Rather than disrupt all work in the Church of the Advent, Grafton gave permission to Fr. Osborne to go on working in the parish. Finally, in this long letter, Fr. Gardner accuses Fr. Benson of deceptive and improper procedures in his dealing with Fr. Grafton. Fr. Benson addressed a letter to Fr. Hall marked "Private, Rev. Father Hall addressed by your mother externally." But the letter within was not from Fr. Hall's mother at all, but a secret communication which Benson did not want Grafton to be aware of. Such a breach of ethics was deeply troubling to Grafton and Gardner and weakened their trust in Benson.

On September 28, 1883, Prescott writes Canon King-Little from Westboro, Mass.[224] (Perhaps Prescott had traveled east to attend the General Convention which was to convene on October 3 in Philadelphia.) Prescott encloses to Canon King-Little a copy of a letter from Fr. Gardner to Fr. Benson reviewing the present difficulties in the Society in America. This could well have been Gardner's long letter of March 15, 1883, but not the printed publication which included a second letter dated October 10. Prescott urges King-Little to take care not to commit himself publicly to either side in what is becoming a serious controversy.

Grafton wrote Prescott from Boston on November 5, 1884 urging Prescott to leave Ripon on January 1 and come to Boston for six months "and let us start together."[225] Probably Grafton means start forming our new monastic community and living and working together. Grafton then adds, "Fr. Gardner's objection makes me fear that he has rather lost heart in the Life" which must also refer to the religious life of their community. Grafton continues:

> If God prospers us and means come in, we may see the way
> in a few years to give up the parishes and find some house
> in the country, or to our having one house in the East and
> West . . . I am bound to the Life, and in some way mean to
> have it. We came out from the S.S.J.E. not because we meant
> to give up our Religious Life, but because F.B. (Fr. Benson)
> would not carry out his agreement.

Grafton has also talked with Bishop Paddock of Massachusetts about this.

A second convergence between the life of Fr. Prescott and Fr. James Huntington occurred on November 25, 1884 when Bishop Henry C. Potter, the Assistant Bishop of New York, heard Huntington's profession of life vows in the newly-formed Order of the Holy Cross. Present were forty-one priests, all the Sisters of St. John the Baptist (in whose chapel the service took place), and three bishops—Quintard of Tennessee, Huntington of Central New York, (James's father) and Bishop Potter. Dr. Houghton, the Rector of the Church of the Transfiguration in New York, was the preacher and spiritual director of the newly founded Order of the Holy Cross. Prescott's sister, Emily, must have been there with the other Sisters of St. John the Baptist. It is hard to believe that she did not share news of this event with her brother in Wisconsin.[226]

There are several letters extant which Prescott wrote from Ripon in December 1884 in which he tries to recover property left by him in Philadelphia.[227] Prescott, replying to an inquiry about a chalice and paten which belonged to the Confraternity of the Blessed Sacrament, writes to Dr. Batterson, the former rector of St. Clement's. Prescott has tried unsuccessfully to secure the return of furniture belonging to his sisters from the Clergy House in Philadelphia. Nearly two years earlier he had also tried to have some books returned which he left in Philadelphia. In his letter to Dr. Batterson, Prescott vents his spleen by referring to Fr. Benson as "General Benson" and to the Cowley fathers in St. Clement's as "his missionary." Prescott concludes, "I think you must see how difficult it is to be concerned with a system in which something called religion is allowed to obscure if not violate morality." Presumably Fr. Benson took the view that inasmuch as Prescott was living under a vow of poverty at the time; any property which he might receive belonged to the Society and not to him personally.

Curiously, although there are in the S.S.J.E. archives in Cambridge five letters written by Prescott to Grafton in January and February 1885, in none of them does Prescott respond to the invitation to come to Boston and spend the next six months there re-establishing their religious community. Instead, Prescott talks about an article in The Living Church, which he considers libelous.[228] Then he talks about a mission in the cathedral in Milwaukee which the Bishop has invited Fr. Maturin and Fr. Hall to conduct and the conditions which the two Cowley fathers placed on their preaching—it would commend sacramental confession and a place must be set up in the cathedral where confessions could be heard. Prescott is certain that the members of the cathedral congregation are not ready for this. In his letter of February 22, Prescott mentions his answer to the earlier article in The Living Church, to which he objected.

Bishop Brown, of Fond du Lac, on March 1 asked Prescott to conduct a Mission in his cathedral church in Fond du Lac.[229] Prescott recommended that he defer the Mission until the cathedral building is finished and then include the Mission as a part of the opening services. The Bishop hopes this can take place in August or September. Prescott told the Bishop that he would like Grafton and Gardner to take part in leading it with him and the Bishop authorized Prescott to invite them on his behalf.

On March 20, 1885 Prescott wrote the Rev. F. M. Riley expressing at length his view of Fr. Benson, which we quote at length.[230]

> I like F. B. Very much in certain ways, but he is a grand puzzle to me. I never met a man with whom acquaintance, as acquaintance goes in the world, was more edifying. He is full of zeal and devotion & he stirs one's better nature like a breath from heaven. I do not see how he could tell a willful lie to save his soul. And yet in carrying out his religious ideas, I cannot recognize him as true or honest, but I think that I knew him to be very immoral indeed . . . Time and time again he has told me that things were so and so when I had proof that they were not & he could have had the same proof if he had been willing to be set right. But no, he had said it, and obedience demanded that what he said should be done & obedience was the duty even if truth was no where. I know dear Riley what I am saying & I know that

I can prove it from letters of F. B.'s to the satisfaction of an irreligious man. This eccentricity of his does not interfere with his being a most delightful companion, & an example in zeal and devotion & I could readily bury the knowledge of his pet crookedness & live a pleasant & profitable life in association with him . . . No religion as I have seen or think I have seen it at work in F. B. is an honor to me, & I can have no place or part in it . . . Mind you, Just here, I am not saying that F. B. is not a saint but granting that he is, he is a saint with a mission & that mission he thinks must be carried out without regard to things honest or lovely or of good report. I do not quarrel with him now for this, it is so human. But I am averse to associate myself with him in it, & if I were, seeing it as I do, I would be both weak & wicked if I were to yield to it. OSP

On April 12, Prescott writes Grafton from Ripon to the effect that a Mission which he conducted in Indianapolis was both disappointing and also satisfactory.[231] But, the story is too long to write and will keep until Prescott sees Grafton. Then Prescott says that Gardner has declined a call to a church in St. Louis and Prescott wonders whether this parish might be right for him. He asks Grafton to mention his name in that regard. Prescott has decided "not to remain here another winter unless I am compelled to do so." He has written this to one or two bishops. Then Prescott reports on the life of his parish in Ripon.

Spiritually, this Parish is making real progress but we are suffering so much from removals that unless a change occurs, of which there is no prospect, the Parish must collapse. We have had a good Lent and I expect to administer baptism to from eight to twelve candidates between this and Easter. I also have a good class for confirmation. Everything looks promising except the finances. My salary is nominally $1,000 and this Parish is behind one-half of that amount.

Grafton continued thinking and talking about an American religious community. He had founded in 1882 the Sisterhood of the Holy Nativity to assist in the ministry of the Church of the Advent. In mid-August 1885, he published an article describing his vision of an American community of clergy and laymen dedicated in the religious life.[232] Grafton listed six requirements for such a society: 1) It must not be an imitation or attempted reproduction of anything in the past; 2) the society must be an American one; 3) if it is to succeed it must grow out of the real wants of the church and be able to meet them; 4) it should have episcopal approval; 5) in its teaching, it should be loyal to the church (by which he means the Episcopal Church); 6) it should have its own definite spirit. Meanwhile, Grafton, Prescott and Gardner were no closer to living the religious life in community than they had been.

Prescott wrote to Grafton from Ripon about plans for a retreat and mission which they had agreed to do together in Advent at the Church of the Redeemer in New York.[233] Prescott, now 61 years old, is beginning to feel his years.

I must have the better part of two days for rest after my journey East and I must get three or four days between the Retreat and the Mission for I cannot begin either fagged by work or travel. I am not nearly so young as I was at forty-five, nor can I do things so rapidly as I could then.

Added to this are financial worries.

> I should be obliged to have a remittance of a portion of my
> expenses before I left Ripon for I am living from hand to
> mouth in a way which never fell to me before. I have received
> from the Parish for this six months ending the first of October
> exactly $300 and out of that I have wound up Allen's life at
> Nashotah, paid his expenses East and established him at the
> Gen. Theo. Sem. in New York. It has been done with great
> economy and he has had his allowance up to the first of next
> month. I never was so poor before, but I never was able to
> give anything like so much away proportionally and I never
> felt happier or for the least part unsatisfied.

Prescott was virtually living in apostolic poverty! Allen was
Prescott's nephew, the son of his late brother, William, who had died in
February 1882. Allen had prepared for seminary at Nashotah House in
Wisconsin and had entered the General Theological Seminary in New
York in the fall of 1885. Allen was ordained priest by Bishop Potter of
New York and then went to serve a church in Westfield, Mass.

In 1886, Prescott resigned as rector of St. Peter's Church, Ripon.
However, he remained canonically resident in the Diocese of Fond du
Lac serving as its General Missionary. He was also a Clerical Deputy
from Fond du Lac it to the General Convention of the Church which met
in Chicago from October 6 to October 28. Virtually no correspondence
survives from either Prescott or Grafton for this year.

However, four letters from Grafton to Prescott, written in 1887
are included in Grafton's published correspondence. In them, Grafton

expresses a continuing desire to re-establish their religious community.
Grafton writes Prescott on May 19 from Boston:

> I write on a venture, not knowing where you are or how to
> get at you. Father Gardner told me yesterday he was going
> back to the East the last of June. The idea that we are not
> going on together, or not seemingly so, is a hard blow to the
> Mother, a hard blow to her faith in our church.[234]

Is "the Mother" our Lord's Mother, the Blessed Virgin Mary or is it
"Mother Church"? Grafton continues:

> I am willing to resign here tomorrow if by so doing we can
> become organized, and you and Gardner think I ought to do
> it. Father Gardner thinks he can wait as well out West as
> here, and it is very trying for him to be here . . . Everything
> regarding the future of the Sisterhood is most bright, and the
> two societies might grow up strong and be a help to each
> other.

The "Sisterhood," of course, is the Sisters of the Holy Nativity
which Grafton founded in Boston in 1882.

Prescott wrote Grafton from Fond du Lac on May 27, 1887
saying:

> Fr. Gardner's leaving 22 Staniford Street certainly knocks
> in the head all possibility of our organizations under the
> Constitution on which we have agreed and I do not believe
> that it would be possible for us to agree upon any other. I

am afloat and nowhere. Our Constitution provides that no member of the Community shall hold a Rectorship except in very exceptional circumstances and how can we think of organizing under such a Constitution while only one of us does not hold a rectorship and therefore only one is in a position to organize at all?[235]

Presumably the one of the three not holding a rectorship at that date was Prescott himself. Prescott continues:

It seems to me that we have got to face this fact, i.e. that if God calls us to a community life, he calls us out of parochial life and if he calls us to parochial life (which you and Gardner seem to think), then our thoughts about community life are fond and idle and just becoming snares if not sins . . . Looking back upon the last year, it seems to me that we were drawn together in Boston that we might learn how far apart we really were.

Grafton replied to Prescott on June 1 in an encouraging tone:[236]

Let us fear nothing, hope for everything. I believe God will let us carry out our Religious life to the profit of His Church yet . . . I am quite ready to make a move, for I have no attachment to the Parish which holds me.

When Prescott wrote Grafton on May 27, he said that he was expected in New Haven on June 22 to officiate at his nephew, Allen's, wedding. But Prescott doubted whether he would be able to be there. In his letter of June 18 to Prescott, Grafton indicated that he was sending this letter both to Fond du Lac and to New Haven because he hopes that Prescott has received the remittance and has been able to come on for his nephew's wedding.[237] Obviously, it was the lack of the car fare which Prescott feared would keep him from coming to New Haven and Grafton had generously sent Prescott the money.

Grafton writes on June 18 a final proposal to Gardner and Prescott:

> If you are willing to organize by this autumn, I will come out to Fond du Lac, and we can all take our vows publicly in the Cathedral and assume the name of the Society. According to our Constitution, I can be allowed to remain here, by your and Father G.'s consent, until we agree that the changed condition of affairs allow of a termination of the relation. So with Father G's newly undertaken work at Plymouth, we can agree that he take it. It will be necessary that you and I should be together, as I wrote you. You to come by the first of September, and remain till July or at the least till January 1st. We can then together get up our Rule and prepare for western work. You can return to take charge of the associated Mission there, while I give myself more especially to the Sisterhood.

Grafton's plan seems clear. Gardner could go to Plymouth, Wisconsin, a town east of Fond du Lac, while Prescott came to Boston to live and work with Grafton for at least four months and preferably longer. At the end of that time, the three would meet in Fond du Lac and publicly take their vows in the Cathedral, Grafton having resigned as rector of the Church of the Advent. But Prescott did not come to Boston in the fall of 1887 and no other letters from him written in 1887 survive. Was Prescott, at age 63, and Grafton at 57, just too old to begin again and re-establish their religious community?

Prescott did write to Grafton on May 22, 1888 from St. Monica's House in Fond du Lac.[238] He had been in Boston from pre-Lent until Easter that year doing pulpit work for Grafton at the Advent. Prescott, still short of money, writes Grafton that he was "counting on receiving a hundred dollars from you . . . and that he should be glad if you would send me a check for whatever you thought was due me from you." This is for Prescott a very unpleasant and offensive matter to write about.

In April 1888, Grafton resigned as rector of the Church of the Advent, as he had written Prescott the previous June that he intended to do, so that he could devote himself to looking after the Sisterhood of the Holy Nativity. He had served the parish for sixteen years, the longest tenure of any of its clergy to date. During these years the new building on Brimmer Street had been erected and the parish had grown from two hundred and fifty to six hundred members.[239] He was widely known and respected not only in Boston, but far beyond.

Then, on May 2, 1888 Bishop Brown, the first Bishop of Fond du Lac, unexpectedly died of pneumonia. Prescott commented on this in his letter of May 22 to Grafton.[240]

> Am in such anxiety and perplexity over the future of this Diocese. I am afraid that it will be very difficult for the clergy and laity to agree upon any man and the first favorite of each body will probably go to the wall.

Six letters from Prescott in Fond du Lac are preserved in the S.S.J.E. archives, letters all written within three weeks.[241] In the first, written on May 26 to Grafton, Prescott advises Grafton that if he can be elected on the first, second or third ballots, then well enough. But Prescott fears a deadlock with the clergy on one side and the laity on the other with the result that there will be no election or else that a poor candidate will be elected. Prescott concludes:

> I am thinking of going East soon after this Council. I am not
> well and I have a longing to get to New Haven again. The
> Bishop's death blocks all action in regard to a community . . .
> and an associate mission for this time being. While the time
> had not come for it, will the time ever come for anything?

We note in Prescott's last sentence the tone of discouragement and apprehension that perhaps their beloved religious community would never be revived.

On the first of June, Prescott writes Grafton that he has learned that Grafton has indicated his willingness to accept if he is elected. Prescott says that the rallying cry of the laity in the Diocese is "The Fathers must not be allowed to run this Diocese."

Prescott writes Grafton further about the upcoming Diocesan election on June 4 explaining that while he does have some influence in the Diocese, he has "nothing approaching to a controlling influence with the laity." Prescott adds:

> As between you and Fiske feeling assured that with you I
> must lose and with Fiske I should win. I should not hesitate
> to go with and for the latter. I do not think you would live

a year if you were to do the work of this Diocese with a moderate devotion. The Diocese is as large as all New England, leaving out one-third of the State of Maine. The work is tough work, traveling and accommodations hard and it would have been cruel for us to ask you to undertake the charge of it. Humanly speaking, Fiske's election puts off another election twenty years beyond what your election would. Though, of course, it is possible that you may be at work when he sleeps.

Because there are many European immigrants in the Diocese, Fiske's ability to preach in German, French and Italian is seen as a distinct asset.

The Rev. George M. Fiske, rector of St. Stephen's Church in Providence, was elected bishop by the Diocese of Fond du Lac on June 6 and Prescott was authorized to write him the news of his election.[242]

The day after the election, Prescott wrote to a friend named "Fay" (spelling?) that "humanly speaking, Fr. Grafton was never a possibility."[243] Prescott gave Grafton his "passive help" until it was demonstrated that there was nothing to be done of help to him. Prescott felt that Fiske was better qualified then any man in the Church.

A week after the election, Prescott wrote Grafton commiserating with him on his loss of the Episcopal election:

> You had only twelve lay votes out of forty odd and no influence of mine, no matter what any one may say to the contrary, could have secured you any more . . . Well, it is all over now. We hope Fiske will accept, that he will be consecrated in his Cathedral and that you will be asked to

preach on this occasion. We are having nice weather just
now and I am deep in garden making.

But Fr. Fiske declined the honor which Fond du Lac had extended
to him. And on November 13, 1888, Fr. Grafton was elected the second
bishop of Fond du Lac.[244] Prescott was in New Haven at the time. The
day after Grafton's election, Prescott wrote him:[245]

> I have just learned from the New York Times of your election
> to Fond du Lac. You know that I did not see my way six
> months ago to advocate your claims, but I congratulate you
> from the bottom of my heart. I honestly did not think the
> result possible and I thought that a strong canvass for you
> would throw the Diocese into the hands of a very moderate,
> if not low, Churchman.

Prescott goes on to say that the illness of Sister Augustine (his
younger sister, Emily) will keep him in the East for the present. Since
his resignation as Rector of St. Peter's Church in Ripon, Prescott has
been serving as General Missionary of the Diocese. He tells Grafton
that he will defer his resignation a while so that he may fill the post
after he takes up his duties as Bishop. Prescott has asked the Rector
of the Church of the Transfiguration in New York, the Rev. George H.
Houghton, for temporary work, but Prescott doubts that anything will
come of it because Dr. Houghton would not be willing to complicate
his relations with the S.S.J.E. by any official connection with him.
However, Prescott adds, he stays at Dr. Houghton's house and works in
his church when he is in New York.

On December 31, 1888, Prescott's older brother, Harry, died in New Haven at the age of 77. Nine days later, Prescott's younger sister, Emily (Sister Augustine) died in the Convent of the Community of St. John the Baptist in New York City just a few days before her 62nd birthday. Prescott wrote Grafton on January 24:[246]

> Thank you very much for your letter which came to me yesterday. It is indeed a great joy to me that my sister died in the habit of a religious. I wish my last end might be like hers. The death of Harry and Emily compels me to remain at the East for the present.

Then, rather pointedly, he concludes, "and, of course, I have no duty elsewhere."

On March 14, Prescott writes Grafton from the Church of the Transfiguration in New York and says:[247]

> I have just heard that your election to the Episcopate of Fond du Lac has been confirmed by the Bishops. I congratulate you and wish you all manner of success in your difficult, but grand future. I do not think I have thanked you for your letter of sympathy on the death of my sister . . . God has been most good to me in giving me work in the absence from Fond du Lac which He still makes necessary.

Apparently Prescott feels that his removal from Wisconsin has nothing to do with himself, but is God's doing.

Four days later, Prescott wrote from New York City to a fellow priest, presumably of the Diocese of Fond du Lac.[248] Someone had sent Prescott a letter stating:

> You ought to know that a report has come into the diocese
> that the opposition in Minnesota to Fr. Grafton's confirmation
> was caused by letters which you wrote into that diocese . . . I
> do feel for you that you should have stirred up so much harsh
> criticism of yourself here in this diocese.

Typically, Prescott wants to know the meaning of this report and whether the priest to whom he is writing can contradict it. Further, Prescott asks the priest to speak to other members of the Standing Committee in an informal way, or share Prescott's letter with them.

Grafton, now the bishop-elect of Fond du Lac, bid farewell to his former congregation at the Church of the Advent at a service on April 13 at which he was the celebrant and Bishop Paddock of Massachusetts the preacher.[249] And on April 25, Grafton was consecrated in St. Paul's Cathedral in Fond du Lac as the second bishop of that Diocese.

On Easter Monday, April 22, 1889—just three days before Grafton's consecration as Bishop of Fond du Lac, Prescott wrote him from New York City, saying "good bye" to his friend of forty years. Because of its significance for their longstanding relationship, the letter warrants publication in full.[250]

> Dear Fr. Grafton:
>
> I did not expect an acknowledgment of my greeting &
> farewell. For the last six or eight months I have seen you

striking off from the path along which for so many years we have gone together, & recognizing the fact that it (?) was reached when you would pass out of sight I felt impelled to call after you "Good bye." And if you had left it there, as you have all the letters which I have written you since I came East you would not be bothered with this.

I have not been unmindful of the fact that for a long time our intimacy has bored you. You were averse to my return to America when I came to Philadelphia. You were pleased, for personal reasons when I made a home for myself in the West. When I went back to Ripon after our exchange of a month I found upon my table a sheet of paper on which you had recorded your resumes in men for founding a community of Priests & after my name you had written "Wont come & I don't want him."

I took no notice of this, for I knew how often I felt irritated at you & was not surprised at your feeling the same about me. But I thought God had some purpose to accomplish by us together & let it pass. I sometime ago lost this illusion. Gardner positively declined looking in that direction so that he was out of it. You were elected to Fond du Lac & that took you out of it. All thought that we were to do anything together was destroyed by these facts & I have accepted it with all its consequences.

If you regard your election as an "offer of God to profess you" I think you are fighting against facts. You say, "It is all of God's ordering" I might agree with you, if Brimmer St. had not had so much to do with it & the Post Office been so largely an agent of material help to the Diocese—the prevailing and deciding argument.

When Bp. Brown died & your name got talked about, you wrote to me & asked me "to pray that you might not be elected." When I voted for Fiske, you wrote & rebuked me for not voting for you, as if you expected me to pray for one thing & try to bring about another.

After your election I congratulated you on the attainment of your wishes & that my letter was received I heard by way of Fond du Lac, it being mentioned as an evidence of my insincerity. I have received a letter from the Rev'd. Mother in regard to something I wrote you & thereby know that letters were received. And now comes your letter which I am acknowledging.

While our intimacy is ended, I hope to retain you in my heart & it seems to me that I am more likely to do this if my good bye be good bye till God shall let us meet where misunderstandings have no place. I will try to think only of that for which I have to thank God in our friendship.

That God may give you success in all your efforts for His glory is my prayer. Good bye.

Yours ever and ever.

OSP

It is clear that Prescott thought Grafton was duplicitous in asking Prescott, on the one hand, to pray that he might not be elected bishop, and then rebuking Prescott for not having voted for him. It is also clear that with Grafton's consecration as bishop, all hopes of reviving their monastic community were at an end. We may wonder, at the same time, why Prescott did not respond to Grafton's repeated invitations to come East for several months so that they could begin re-establishing their community. But it is typical of Prescott in the end to act decisively, to make in this courteous but firm way, a clean break with Grafton. Many times before in his life when he was faced with a situation which he deemed intolerable, or incompatible with his principles, Prescott acted decisively—painful as that action was. And surely, this must have been a painful break to make. But where a principle was at stake Prescott could not temporize, could not compromise, could not take the path of polite expediency. And so, his long, loving relationship with Grafton came to an end.

A brief note informing Grafton that Prescott is now an Assistant Minister at the Church of the Transfiguration in New York, written on October 26, and requesting his letter dimissory to be sent from Fond du Lac to the Bishop of New York serves as a formal termination to a relationship of forty years.[251]

LAST YEARS: NEW YORK AND CONNECTICUT

When Prescott became the Assistant Minister at the Church of the Transfiguration in New York City, it was a parish of about 600 communicants.[252] It offered a daily celebration of the Holy Communion and a second celebration on Sundays and other holy days. In 1889, it reported 105 baptisms, 29 persons confirmed, and 75 burials. Dr. Houghton, its founding rector, had served there since the parish began in 1848 and was now 69 years old. There was certainly plenty of work for an Assistant Minister to do. Prescott remained there in this position for three years.

118

In the summer of 1889, Prescott wrote a will leaving all which he possessed to his sister, Mary Rebecca, of New Haven.[253] The will was dated June 13 and signed at the Church of the Transfiguration.

There are two cordial letters to Prescott from Fr. Robert Lay Page S.S.J.E., who succeeded Fr. Benson as Superior of the S.S.J.E. in 1890.[254] Fr. Page thinks he left his manuscript book with notes on the Passion in his room at Dr. Houghton's. Page says that things are looking up for the Society and then speaks of several new members in it.

Prescott saved a charming letter written to him on December 10, 1890 from an old friend, the Rev. John Baghot Dela Bere, vicar of Buxted St. Mary's in Sussex.[255] He is happy that Prescott is in "peaceful and congenial work." He asks his children if they remember Fr. Prescott to which his 25 year old daughter, Bridget, replies, "Oh yes, fat and fatherly!" The vicar assures Prescott that he has his "life-long gratitude and prayers" for his ministry many years ago.

Sometime late in 1889, Prescott preached a sermon at the Church of the Transfiguration on St. Peter's instruction to Cornelius and his kinsfolk (Acts 10: 36-44). Early in 1890, Prescott published this sermon which he entitled, "Apostolic Conditions to Church Communion." with a dedication to his rector, Dr. Houghton "with much affection."[256]

In 1890, Fr. Gardner became the President of Nashotah House in Wisconsin, having served as General Superintendent of Missions in the Diocese of Fond du Lac after Prescott's resignation. Fr. Gardner continued as President of Nashotah House until 1897.

Prescott saved a letter he received from H.W. Fay, written February 9, 1891.[257] In it Fay comments on Gardner's successful fundraising on behalf of Nashotah House. He also mentions a mission which Prescott is to conduct somewhere in Delaware. Fay observed:

> The times do change, sure enough. Evangelicalism is gone, and with it some of the beliefs dear at old time to the pious heart. Where is Satan, for instance, and hell-fire and Augustinianism generally? Gone to India with the last Englishman who took them seriously.

"The last Englishman" is probably an allusion to Fr. Benson who traveled to India after stepping down as Superior of the Society.

Prescott wrote from New York on November 21, 1891 to "My dear Doctor" but the recipient's name is not known.[258] Prescott explains that his use of the word "unprincipled" with reference to Fr. Benson's actions towards the American priests of the Society was "carefully chosen to express exactly what I meant." Fr. Benson's position, writes Prescott, "was that of the present Emperor of Germany, 'My will is the supreme law.' 'The Constitution of the Society (so he wrote) is what I say.'"

There is one further convergence between Prescott and Fr. Huntington and the young Order of the Holy Cross. During the years that Prescott served as Assistant Minister at the Transfiguration, the tiny Holy Cross community was living in a house at 417 Pleasant Avenue in Harlem.[259] Dr. Houghton was also the spiritual advisor of the Order. We may assume that he and Prescott discussed this new American monastic community, a matter of such long-standing concern to Prescott. In 1892, the house in Harlem which the Holy Cross fathers occupied was sold and they started looking for a new home. By a remarkable coincidence, Miss Lucretia Van Bibber, Prescott's old friend and parishioner from the Church of the Ascension in Westminster, MD, offered to the All Saints Sisters in Baltimore a large house next to the parish church in Westminster. The Sisters declined the offer. But the Mother Superior, knowing of the Holy Cross fathers' need for housing, suggested that

Miss Van Bibber offer her house to them, which she did. In August 1892, the three young priests of the Order of the Holy Cross moved into Prescott's former parish. It is scarcely credible that Prescott was unaware of all this. But there is no trace of any correspondence or other communication between Prescott and the Holy Cross fathers. Next door to the house in Harlem, which the Holy Cross fathers had occupied, was the home of Brother Gilbert and the Brothers of Nazareth who were to provide a home and nursing care for Prescott in the last years of his life.

For a short time in 1893, after leaving the Church of the Transfiguration, Prescott served as temporary curate in the Church of the Holy Innocents in Hoboken, New Jersey.[260]

In the fall of 1893, Prescott wrote Bishop Williams of Connecticut offering his services at St. Luke's Church in New Haven. St. Luke's was an African-American congregation which had been established in 1844, one of the first for persons of color in the Episcopal Church.[261] Trinity Church, New Haven, and its able rector, Dr. Harry Croswell, had played a large part in its foundation. The parish was served from 1884 to March 1891 by the Rev. Alfred C. Brown, a native of Santa Cruz in the West Indies. Fr. Brown was popular and during his years as rector St. Luke's grew, a chancel was added to the building and $2,000 had been raised to free the building of debt. On December 7, 1886 Bishop Williams consecrated the church building which was located on Park Street, between Chapel and Crown streets in New Haven. Since Fr. Brown's departure, the parish had been without a resident priest.

Although Bishop Williams was strenuously opposed to the ritualism for which Prescott was well known, he was happy to receive his proposal to serve St. Luke's. The number of African-American priests was extremely limited. In the racially segregated church life of the 1890's, Prescott's influence as an Anglo-Catholic ritualist would be strictly limited to St. Luke's parish itself. Accordingly, the Bishop wrote Prescott on September 18, 1893.[262]

> It gives me pleasure to comply with your request and I will add that I will second it gladly. St. Luke's is a financial worry and I shall be thankful if they will put themselves into your hands. All colored people are "kittle cattle," as they say in Scotland, and need gentle dealing.

Webster's Unabridged Dictionary defines the expression, "kittle cattle" as meaning "difficult to manage, to get on with or to depend on."

Perhaps the Bishop hoped that Prescott would go easy on introducing Catholic ceremonial in St. Luke's parish. On December 1, 1893 Prescott assumed his duties as rector of St. Luke's Church at an annual salary of $425.

Prescott was no stranger to St. Luke's. In the fall of 1866, while he was serving Christ Church in West Haven, CT., Prescott offered to conduct a service on Wednesdays at St. Luke's, which was without a rector. His offer provoked much discussion at the November 16 meeting of St. Luke's Vestry, which decided to accept his offer. We remember, also, that in 1879 Prescott had written to another priest expressing his great admiration for the Right Rev. James T. Holly, who had served St. Luke's from 1855 to 1865 and was the Bishop of Haiti from 1874 to his death in 1911.[263] Prescott wrote his priest correspondent in 1879, "I take very great interest in your people"—presumably persons of color. Prescott concluded that letter "for your race's sake I will do what I can to forward your work." From the time he began his ministry at St. Clement's, Prescott and the clergy working there with him had ministered to a number of African-Americans. Prescott's efforts to secure the permission of his Episcopal neighbors to renting a hall in the western part of the city were frustrated by his neighbors' refusal.

In spite of what Prescott had written Grafton the previous April, Grafton wrote a gracious letter to Prescott on January 1, 1894.[264] He said:

> It is a very blessed work you have undertaken. Gardner and myself were talking about it the other day at Nashotah. We never meet but we speak of you.

And on January 16, Bishop Williams accepted Prescott's letter dimissory from the diocese of New York.[265]

As might be expected, Prescott promptly introduced Catholic ceremonies and traditional appointments into the liturgy at St. Luke's. Some of the parishioners welcomed this. In June 1894, one lady gave an altar cross. On Easter Day 1896, a processional cross was given by another lady in the parish. But some of the Vestrymen were opposed, as a later rector of the parish recalled forty years later:[266]

> It was during Father Prescott's rectorship that certain innovations in the parish's church life were started which more or less continued to the present. Candles were placed on the altar for the first time. Some of the colored vestrymen felt

the presence of candlesticks was contrary to the traditions of
Connecticut churchmanship and proceeded to remove them.
Today, these same candlesticks are on the altar but one of
them still bears the marks of battle incurred when at one of
the vestry meetings, it was forcibly snatched from the altar.

On St. Luke's Day, October 18, 1894, the parish celebrated the
fiftieth anniversary of its founding. Bishop Williams was present and
presided. And Prescott's former colleague in the S.S.J.E., Arthur C.A.
Hall, was the preacher. Hall had been elected Bishop of Vermont in
the fall of 1893 and the Society had released him from his vows. He
was consecrated a bishop in the Cathedral in Burlington, Vermont
on February 2, 1894, the second former Cowley father to serve as a
bishop in a diocese of the American Episcopal Church. St. Luke's
parish used this occasion to establish a building fund which resulted in
the construction of a new church building on Whalley Avenue in New
Haven eleven years later.

On his return to New Haven, Prescott established a home in West
Haven for his sister, Mary, and their niece, Alida T. Prescott. She was
the daughter of their brother, William, who had died in 1882. A year
later, the three Prescotts moved back in to New Haven at an address on
Crown Street near St. Luke's Church. This was to be Fr. Prescott's last
home in New Haven.[267]

Early in 1895, Prescott wrote a letter, which has not survived, to
Bishop Williams inquiring, it would seem, about the orthodoxy of the
teaching in a Pastoral Letter issued by the House of Bishops. Bishop
Williams replied on March 1 explaining the process by which the
Letter was drafted dealing with the Incarnation and with (Biblical)
inspiration.[268] The Bishop explains that the Letter was the utterance of

the Episcopate who was in full accord with it doctrinally. Bishop says that no clergyman is <u>compelled</u> to read these Pastoral Letters. Only letters issued at the time of a General Convention must be read to each parish. Bishop Williams closes by writing, "If I were you I would say nothing more about it."

Prescott saved a letter written on September 16, 1896 by Fr. W. H. Longridge from the Mission House of the S.S.J.E. in Boston.[269] It was apparently in response to an invitation from Prescott for Fr. Field to come to New Haven probably for a Mission. It may be that Prescott saved this letter because Fr. Longridge, who had just returned from England, speaks of the beautiful new church at Cowley, even though it is still unfinished.

Bishop Grafton wrote to Prescott on April 26, 1897 sending cordial Easter greetings.[270] Grafton is preparing to attend the fourth Lambeth Conference which was held later that year and he has been appointed one of four speakers on "The Relation of Religious Orders to the Episcopate." The Bishop writes, "I very naturally ask you to give me the help of your wisdom and wide experience." Grafton then asks, "is there not a difference between Clerical orders and those like Sisterhoods?" Grafton signs himself, "Your old friend." We do not have Prescott's reply.

In 1897, the Rev. Chauncey B. Brewster was elected Bishop Coadjutor of Connecticut. Brewster had been married twice. His first wife died in 1885 and in 1893 he re-married. Prescott considered Brewster's second marriage to be an impediment to his consecration as a bishop. Prescott was mindful of the scriptural injunction, "Now a bishop must be above reproach, married only once" (I Timothy 3: 2a). Accordingly, Prescott wrote Brewster:[271]

> I wish I knew some form of words in which to address you
> without running the risk of seeming to be rude and to be
> brief without being brusque. Ever since my first rectorship
> under Bishop Whittingham, I have believed that a second
> marriage is forbidden to a man in Holy Orders, and following
> his example, I do not see how I can have part or lot in the
> service of the 28th inst. So soon as St. Luke's comes under
> your jurisdiction as Bishop Coadjutor, it is plainly my duty
> to give you reverent obedience and the utmost respect and
> honor in all our official relations.

In keeping with this stance, Prescott wrote Mr. Burton Mansfield, the Secretary of the Committee on Arrangements for the Consecration declining appointment to this Committee and asking that his name be removed from the list "without delay."[272]

Prescott also wrote on October 7 to the Rt. Rev. Edward S. Talbot, Bishop of Rochester in England whom he understood was going to assist in the consecration of Brewster.[273] Prescott writes:

> I think that you ought to know that some of us feel very
> acutely the scandal of the election of a digamist (sic) to
> the episcopate and that we should regret exceedingly the
> participation of any one in the consecration who presumes
> would have a (illegible) importance in being regarded as a
> representative of the whole English hierarchy.

Whether Prescott's letter dissuaded Bp. Talbot, or whether he was not planning to attend the consecration we do not know. We only know that he was not one of the participating bishops in Brewster's consecration.

Prescott saved an undated draft of a letter which, from internal evidence, was written in March or April 1897 and addressed to the Wardens and Vestry of St. Luke's, although that address is missing.[274] Prescott speaks of a significant shortfall in his salary payments over the past 18 months. On his monthly salary of $425 he had only received $359.20 of which $10 was a gift from St. Paul's parish. Thus St. Luke's is in arrears on his salary some $278.30. He adds:

> It is the duty of every member of the Parish entitled to a vote to find out where the fault lies and remedy it. The whole future of the Parish is at stake in the Easter meeting, and I beg you gentlemen to face the responsibility which is on you for your race's and church's sake, in the fear of God and without the fear of man.

> I have read this communication to you and shall not leave a copy of it with you for I would rather not have it put on the record, and I should deprecate any circumstances which would compel me to embody what I have written in a letter to the congregation or in an appeal to the Ecclesiastical Authorities of the Diocese.

> May God bless and keep us all and enable us to act always as in His sight and to His glory . . .

In 1896, Prescott's niece, Alida, moved to New York. On April 25, 1899, Alida was married in Christ Church, New Haven to Prescott LeBreton of Buffalo, N.Y.[275] The Rev. George B. Morgan, Rector of Christ Church, and Fr. Prescott officiated at the wedding. In 1899,

Prescott's sister, Mary, moved from their home to the Trinity Church Home nearby. Although Mary had been a lifelong member of Trinity, she had taken part in activities at Christ Church, as had many other members of Trinity during the early years of Christ Church. The Rev. Dr. J. H. Van Deerlin, who was Rector of Christ Church from 1884 to 1886, recalled that "among the women who were especially faithful and helpful were Miss Edwards, Miss Linzee and Miss Prescott, the sister of Fr. Oliver Prescott."[276]

In July, 1898 the new building of Christ Church, New Haven was dedicated by Bp. Brewster. Fr. Prescott served as the Epistler at the service.

Finally, in 1900, at the age of 76, poor health forced Oliver Prescott to resign as Rector of St. Luke's Church. He had served there seven years—the longest tenure of any in the fifty-three years of his ordained ministry!

On February 7, 1899, Bishop Williams died bringing to an end a remarkable career of 45 years as Dean of Berkley Divinity School (of which he was the founder), 48 years as a Bishop, and the last 12 years of his life Presiding Bishop of the Episcopal Church. On Bishop Williams' death, Bishop Brewster became the Bishop of Connecticut. He must have been aware that Prescott had been quite unable to accumulate any money on his very modest salary and accordingly Brewster promptly saw to it that Prescott was voted an annual pension of $200 from the Connecticut Aged and Infirm Clergy Fund, beginning June 1900.[277]

In the file of undated materials relating to Prescott in the General Theological Seminary Library are thirteen pages in Prescott's handwriting of a draft of a rule for the Order of the Brothers of Nazareth.[278] The rule makes ample provision for the approval of the bishop of any diocese to the presence of the order in that diocese. By painful experience Prescott had learned the importance of that requirement. There are additional materials in this file from the Rev. John J.R. Spong, of New York City, who is listed in Lloyd's Clerical Directory as Chaplain of the Order of the Brothers of Nazareth. He and Prescott were evidently collaborating on the Rule for this Order which had been established by Brother Gilbert. The Order of the Brothers of Nazareth started as an adjunct for laymen of the Order of the Holy Cross, which then thought of itself as primarily for priests. Gilbert Tompkins had worked as a layman in Episcopal churches and had entered the novitiate at Cowley, but had not been professed there.[279] In March 1886, Tompkins was admitted as a novice of the Order of the Brothers of Nazareth and a year later, Fr. Huntington received his vows for three years at a service at Holy Cross Mission in New York City. Brother Gilbert established a Convalescent Home for men and boys which was located in Harlem, then a pleasant residential neighborhood. The Hospital was opened in December 1886. In 1889, the Holy Cross community moved into a house near the Convalescent Hospital. In 1890, Brother Gilbert was given a tract of land at Verbank, New York on which a large building was erected to house "convalescent men and boys, old men and chronic sufferers" as their letterhead declared. It was here that Fr. Prescott was to spend the last years of his life. This is the final convergence between him and Fr. James Huntington and the Order of the Holy Cross.

There is preserved in the Library of the General Theological Seminary, a personal pocket diary which Prescott acquired in 1901.[280] He continued using it for the next two years so that it gives a composite picture of the last years of his life. But it is impossible to tell in which year certain events took place. Inside the front cover Prescott left instructions for those who were to be notified "in the event of anything happening by which I should be unable to tell of myself." Among those listed was his nephew, Allen, in Cuba, New York. He asked to be taken to St. Luke's Hospital if he were in New York and if this were convenient. And in the event of his death, he asked that the Rev. A. Ritchie, Rector of St. Ignatius Church in New York City, should be informed. He concluded "May God have mercy on my soul."

He mentions being taken to Grace Hospital in New Haven and also to St. Luke's Hospital in New York City. From there, apparently he went to Heart's Ease Cottage in Nyack. It would seem that by May 1901, he was well enough to travel to Cuba, New York where he spent most of the month with Allen and his wife. On May 22, 1901, he was welcomed by Brother Gilbert to All Saints' Home in Verbank, N.Y. Prescott mentions saying Mass in the Chapel wearing the purple chasuble given him a year ago which he has not been well enough to use. He often mentions writing letters to Polly (his sister, Mary). On August 10, 1901, being the 40th Anniversary of his father's death, he says a requiem for his parents. Obviously, his memory was still good. A few days later he notes having taken the longest walk since he left Cuba, N.Y. The next day he says Mass in reference to the 53rd anniversary of his ordination to the priesthood. But there are also more ominous entries. He notes on February 28 (is the year 1902?) that he had "slight difficulty in talk, articulating, headaches." Then, on Sunday, March 31, he said Mass in the Chapel. "A good deal used up by so doing. Left foot much affected at night." On Sunday, September 15 (again, the year is not known) he said Mass for the community and its work. "I made an attempt to preach at Morning Prayer with the result that I am well convinced that my preaching days are past." He notes the arrival of three boxes of books from New Haven. He notes walks taken to the Village of Blauvelt. Fr. Ritchie brings him the Blessed Sacrament on the anniversary of his second birth in Holy Baptism.

Then, on November 13, 1901 his sister, Mary, died in New Haven at the age of 80. He did not receive the telegram because it was mailed to Verbank so that he was informed of her death the next day, too late to get to New Haven for her funeral. On November 15, Prescott said a mass of requiem for his sister and noted in his diary, "Will of God be done." The next day, a Sunday, he wrote:

> My first Sunday for a long time in which I have not felt that I ought to write to my sister, Polly. It may be that we are nearer to each other than when she was in New Haven. At any rate, I feel that I am nearer her.

The following December 1 he wrote:

> My thoughts have been a good deal with Polly to whom I can no longer send letters. I wonder whether she knows how much I miss her.

In February, 1902 according to the parish records of Christ Church, New Haven Prescott gave the parish a set of black eucharistic vestments to be worn at requiem celebrations

According to The Nazareth Chronicle, published by the Order of the Brothers of Nazareth, at Easter 1902, Prescott made a gift of $45 to the Order.[281] And on November 15 of that same year, Bishop Grafton came to Priory Farm to visit Prescott. It was a gracious thing for the Bishop to do. He also confirmed a class of 13 boys at St. Paul's Training School run by the Order. In 1888, before Grafton was elected Bishop of Fond du Lac, Prescott had expressed the fear that Grafton would not last a year as bishop in that geographically large diocese. But Prescott's dire prediction was wrong. The Bishop was 72 when he visited Prescott at Priory Farm and he was to live ten more years to the age of 82. At Easter 1903, Prescott gave $50 to the Order for the care of patients. At last, on November 17, Prescott died. Four days later he was buried next to his sister Mary in the Grove Street Cemetery in New Haven, where so many of his family were buried. He was 79 at the time of his death. Identical tall white marble tomb stones mark Prescott's grave and that of his sister. Prescott's tombstone bears the inscription "Made a priest in 1848. Father to many souls in America and England." The remaining two lines of his epitaph have eroded on the soft white marble and are no longer legible.

A month later, Brother Gilbert wrote to Mr. J.E. Watkis of Hammonton, New Jersey, who had inquired about Fr. Prescott.[282] He explained that while Prescott had been "more or less feeble" during his two and one-half years at Priory Farm, he had only been confined to his bed or room for the last three or four weeks of his life. Brother Gilbert wrote further:

> He has, however, had frequent attacks of convulsions (a characteristic of Bright's disease), since he came to us, which would prostrate him for several days at a time. He continually grew more and more feeble, and I think for about two months before his death, he hardly recognized any of us; most of the time, however, he was bright and cheerful and bore his sufferings very manfully, notwithstanding his advanced age. Toward the last we were obliged to have nurses in constant attendance and two young men who have been trained in Bellevue Hospital took the best of care of him. He passed

away very peacefully, not a sigh or moan—simply entering into his long rest as one who is weary falls asleep.

In its February 1904 issue, The Nazareth Chronicle carried a brief obituary of Fr. Prescott in which was said:

> He was professed in the S.S.J.E. June 6, 1870. It was his delight when strong enough to daily offer the Holy Sacrifice in the Brothers' Chapel and to join with them in the recitation of the daily offices. A great lover of nature and of rural life, most of his time was spent out of doors when the weather would permit.

Thus Prescott's hope that he might die as his sister Emily did "in the habit of a religious" was very nearly (if not exactly) fulfilled.

In his address to the 1904 Annual Diocesan Convention, Bishop Brewster included this tribute to Prescott.[283]

> Personally acquainted with the leaders and himself prominent among the early adherents, of the "Oxford Movement," Father Prescott was unswervingly faithful to his convictions of Catholic truth. In the face of misunderstanding and opposition he never faltered in what he believed to be his duty. In the more than fifty years of his devoted priesthood he ministered with unusual effect to a great multitude, and many will remember him before God.

What sort of a person was Oliver Sherman Prescott? How may we sum up his character? He was a person whose principles, theological and religious, remained remarkably consistent throughout his life. They were formed under the influence of the <u>Tracts for the Times</u> to which he was introduced by his rector, the Rev. Harry Croswell, and in which he was nurtured at the General Theological Seminary. From his ordination in 1847 to his death fifty-six years later he remained a Catholic Churchman and a dedicated ritualist. Beyond this, Prescott's vocation to the monastic life was clear to him early in his life and remained with him to the end. He was truly called by God, not only to be a priest, but also to exercise his priesthood in a religious community in so far as he could.

Prescott was not an original thinker. He was an activist. He took the ideas formulated by others, particularly the leaders of the Oxford movement, and implemented them, acted on them, lived them. He was a parish priest. He was not a writer of books or tracts. His few surviving sermons are well written but not remarkable for their originality. He chiefly speaks today through his many letters which survive. They are fluent and literate and the product of a good intellect.

He was quick to defend his good name, his prerogatives as a priest and the Catholic principles in which he so strongly believed. He could not let a false rumor or an erroneous statement go unchallenged. He was a valiant champion for the truth, as he perceived it. In the course of these lifelong battles Prescott made many enemies but also won many others. Although he could be charming, he cared very little for worldly advantage. To the contrary, time and again he sacrificed his personal comfort and well being to the cause to which he was so ardently committed. With the author of the Second Letter to Timothy, Fr. Prescott could well have said at his end, "I have fought the good fight, I have finished the race, I have kept the faith."

Just a week after Fr. Prescott's death friends of his meeting in New York City adopted the following resolution in his memory:

At a meeting of the New York Catholic Club held on Nov. 24, 1903 it was unanimously voted that the following resolution be entered upon the minutes of the Club, and published in THE LIVING CHURCH newspaper.

Resolved, That in the life of the Rev. Father Prescott, now gone home to God, we recognize and thank our Heavenly Father for the model of a noble, priestly character.

Perhaps the most conspicuous feature of his ministry was its entire freedom from personal ambition. He seemed to have in his thought nothing but the glory of the Master Christ and the good of His Church. Singularly unselfish he was ever content with the less conspicuous places, doing indeed noble and enduring work wherever he served, yet in almost every case leaving it for others to reap the fruit of that work.

Scarcely less marked a characteristic of Father Prescott's life was his unswerving fidelity throughout the course of a ministry of fifty-six years, to the Catholic religion. Nothing could induce him to abate one iota of what he knew to be the Church's teaching and the Church's practice. This meant throughout his life much hardship for himself, misunderstanding, the alienation of friends, something often very like persecution. But he never faltered in what he felt to be his duty to his Master Christ.

Nor can anyone who was privileged to know much of Father Prescott's ministrations, fail to remember with grateful affection the reality of his teachings in the spiritual life. No mission sermons penetrated more deeply than his, no meditations in retreat more profoundly moved the heart, no dealing with individual penitents in the Confessional was better calculated to promote through amendment, and genuine contrition. We believe that hundreds of souls brought to God by his ministrations will rise up in the last day to call him blessed.

In a word, Father Prescott was a true Catholic priest. What better praise could any man have than that? May his soul rest in peace, and may light perpetual shine upon him.

For the Club:

Arthur Ritchie, G. M. Christian, Charles Mercer Hall, Committee[284]

SOURCES

CDA—   Archives of the Episcopal Diocese of Connecticut, 1335 Asylum Avenue, Hartford, Conn. 06105

GTS—   General Theological Seminary Library, 175 Ninth Avenue, New York, New York 10011

Prescott himself copied and saved letters he had written and which he considered important or to which he may have wished to refer in the future. In addition, he saved a few other letters which he received and some documents. Sometime late in his life Fr. Prescott gave these letters to the Seminary library for safekeeping. Or, he may have left instructions for them to be given to the Seminary after his death. Dated letters have been calendared by the library and are kept in Box 1. Undated correspondence and other undated papers are in Box 2. Most of the letters cited here are dated and are from Box 1. When a document or letter from Box 2 is cited the citation specifies that it is from Box 2.

MDA— Archives of the Episcopal Diocese of Maryland, 4 East University Parkway, Baltimore, Maryland 02111.

Before he became the Bishop of Maryland in 1840, William Whittingham taught church history at the General Theological Seminary in New York City. In his correspondence as bishop he exercised the mind of an historian, saving all the letters he received, noting on each its author, the date it was received and the date he replied to it (or saw the writer, if that was appropriate.) The letters have been catalogued and are a rich resource for the 39 years of Whittingham's episcopate.

MASS— Archives of the Episcopal Diocese of Massachusetts, 138 Tremont Street, Boston, Massachusetts 02111

NHCHS— New Haven Colony Historical Society, library, 114 Whitney Avenue, New Haven, Connecticut 06510.

PDAB— Archives of the Episcopal Diocese of Pennsylvania, housed in the Presbyterian Historical Society, 425 Lombard Street, Philadelphia, Pennsylvania 19147.

SSJE— Archives of the Society of St. John the Evangelist, 980 Memorial Drive, Cambridge, Massachusetts 02138.

It appears that someone in the Society intended writing a biography of Fr. Prescott and to that end gathered and copied letters and other documents from him and to him. That person may have been the Rev. Duncan Convers, SSJE who died in 1929. As a young man Fr. Convers served at St. Clement's Church, Philadelphia when Prescott was its Rector. An undated, unsigned manuscript biography of Prescott is, we assume, by Fr. Convers.

YUL-MA— Yale University Library, Manuscripts and Archives, Sterling Memorial Library, New Haven, Connecticut 06520.

ENDNOTES

1. NHCHS—Microfilm, The Arnold G. Dana Collection A The Prescott Family and Their Homes,@ Vol. 1 p.47.

2. Connecticut State Library—Hartford Probate Court records, reel 909.

3. CDA—Microfilm, Baptismal records of Trinity Church, New Haven, CT.

4. NHCHS—Microfilm, op cit.

5. NHCHS—New Haven City Directory for 1840.

6. YUL-MA—Rev. Harry Croswell Diary, Vol.2 p.16 March 4, 1825.

7. Trinity College, Hartford, CT. Registrar's records.

8. YUL-MA—Catalog of the officers and students in Yale College.

9. YUL-MA—Minutes of Brothers in Unity for Academical Years 1842-43.

10. YUL-MA—Croswell Diary, Vol. 7, p. 259-60, May 28, 1843.

11. YUL-MA—Ibid. Vol. 7, p.479, August 5, 1844.

12. YUL-MA—Ibid. Vol. 8, p.225-6, November 28, 1845.

13. YUL-MA—Ibid. Vol. 8, p.471, July 21, 1847.

14. SSJE Archives—Unsigned, undated manuscript biography of Prescott.

15. GTS—Prescott File #7, W.C. to dear friend, Boston, August 13, 1847.

16. GTS—William Glenney French, History of the Order of the Holy Cross at Valle Crucis, North Carolina under Rt. Rev. Levi Silliman Ives, 1847-1851, unpublished manuscript.

17. GTS—French, op. cit.

18. GTS—French, ibid.

19. Sister Hilary, CSM, The Society of the Holy Cross, in Holy Cross Magazine, published by the Order of the Holy Cross, July 1945.

20. Michael T. Malone, Levi Silliman Ives, Tractarian and Roman Catholic Convert, Unpublished Ph.D. Thesis, Duke University, 1950.

21. GTS—File of Bishops' Papers, quoted in Malone, op. cit.

22. MDA—Prescott papers.

23. GTS—File of Bishops' Letters.

24. YUL-MA—Croswell Diary, Vol. 9, p.80, August 12, 1848.

25. YUL-MA—Ibid. Vol.9, p.80, August 13, 1848.

26. Episcopal Diocese of North Carolina, Journal of Convention, 1847.

27. MASS—Massachusetts Diocesan Journal, 1850.

28. MASS—ibid. Journal, 1851.

29. Michael T. Malone, "The Ecclesiastical Trials in Massachusetts of Oliver Sherman Prescott. Church History, 1972, pp. 94-107. This is an excellent, detailed description of the four trials.

30. YUL-MA—Croswell Diary, Vol. 10, p. 114, February 10, 1851.

31. YUL-MA—Baldwin Family Papers, 1851-1852, Apr. Group #55, Box #30.

32. SSJE—Prescott to French, April 14, 1851.

33. Michael Malone, op. cit.

34. MDA—Prescott to Whittingham, November 15, 1851.

35. MDA—Dana to Whittingham, November 18, 1851.

36. GTS—Prescott Files, #2 printed letter to Bishop Eastburn, Sept. 25, 1851.

37. GTS—Bishops' Papers, Ives to Prescott.

38. Michael Malone, op. cit., p. 102 quoting from the Churchman, March 13, 1851.

39. SSJE—Prescott File, "Mr. Dana's Argument in the Prescott Case," from the Churchman.

40. Ibid.

41. MASS—Trial of the Rev. O.S. Prescott, a Presbyter of the Diocese of Massachusetts on Charges of Heresy, etc., Cambridge, Metcalf & Co., 1851, p. 12.

42. Ibid.

43. Lucid, R.F., editor, The Journal of Richard Henry Dana, Jr., Cambridge, The Belknap Press of Harvard Univ., 1968, vol. II, p. 481.

44. MDA—Prescott to Whittingham, May 5, 1852.

45. Lucid, op. cit., p. 490.

46. Ibid., p. 491.

47. Ibid., p. 483.

48. MDA—Prescott to Whittingham, January 7, 1853.

49. MDA—Pusey to Prescott, November 12, 1852.

50. Ibid.

51. MDA—Prescott to Whittingham, October 12, 1853.

52. The full text of Prescott's Memorial is reprinted in <u>A Forgotten Memorial</u>, by Rev. Duncan Convers, SSJE, in the American Church Monthly, Dec., 1921.

53. MDA—Letter Dimissory from Bishop Eastburn to Whittingham, Nov. 2, 1853.

54. SSJE—Prescott File, Whittingham to Prescott, Dec. 16, 1853.

55. Quoted in Grafton, Charles C., <u>A Journey Godward</u>, pp. 77-78.

56. MDA—Miss L. Van Bibber to Whittingham, Oct. 11, 1853.

57. SSJE—Prescott File, typed copy of letter from Whittingham to Prescott, November 9, 1853.

58. MDA—Prescott to Whittingham, November 7, 1853.

59. SSJE—Prescott File, op. cit., November 9, 1853.

60. MDA—Prescott to Whittingham, August 15, 1854.

61. William K. Tinkham, "Grafton: Priest and Author," in <u>The Beacon</u>, Michaelmas, 1988, published by the Church of the Advent, Boston.

62. Ibid.

63. MDA—Prescott to Whittingham, April 19, 1855.

64. Ibid.

65. MDA—Prescott to Whittingham, July 17, 1856.

66. MDA—Prescott to Whittingham, February 2, 1857.

67. MDA—Bound pamphlets, vol. 18, no. 32.

68. MDA—Bishop Potter to Whittingham, April 1, 1857.

69. MDA—Prescott to Whittingham, March 6, 1858.

70. MDA—Prescott to Whittingham, July 12, 1858.

71. MDA—Prescott to Whittingham, July 26, 1858.

72. MDA—Prescott to Whittingham, September 17, 1858.

73. MDA—Prescott to Whittingham, November 3, 1858.

74. MDA—Prescott to Whittingham, June 20, 1859.

75. MDA—Prescott to Whittingham, August 20, 1859.

76. MDA—Prescott to Whittingham, August 29, 1859.

77. MDA—Prescott to Whittingham, November 2, 1859.

78. MDA—Prescott to Whittingham, January 31, 1860, enclosing a copy of Archer's letter to Prescott of January 24, 1860.

79. Vestry Minutes, St Peter's Church, Ellicott City, MD.

80. GTS—Prescott File #4, Prescott to his sisters, June 15, 1860.

81. MDA—Prescott to Whittingham, July 9, 1860.

82. GTS—Prescott File #5, Prescott to his sisters, July 22, 1860.

83. MDA—T. Harwood Perine to Whittingham, November 5, 1860.

84. MDA—Prescott to Whittingham, January 8, 1861.

85. MDA—Hunter to Whittingham, March 25, 1861.

86. GTS—Prescott File #54, Prescott to his sister, Second Sunday in Lent, 1861.

87. MDA—Prescott to Whittingham, May 21, 1861.

88. George Champlin Mason, Annals of Trinity Church, Newport, vol. II, 1821-1892, pub. 1894, p. 226.

89. MDA—Prescott to Whittingham, June 24, 1861.

90. Mason, op. cit., p. 227.

91. Trinity Church, New Haven, Ct. Parish records.

92. New Haven County Probate Court Records, Connecticut State Library, Hartford.

93. MDA—Prescott to Whittingham, September 6, 1861.

94. MDA—Prescott to Whittingham, October 15, 1861.

95. MDA—Dr. J. D. Oden to Whittingham, October 12, 1861.

96. MDA—Prescott to Whittingham, undated but received November 14, 1861.

97. MDA—Prescott to Whittingham, November 14, 1861.

98. Mason, op. cit., p. 239.

99. MDA—Prescott to Whittingham, April 22, 1862.

100. Mason, op. cit., p. 244.

101. Prescott File, Alumni records, Trinity College, Hartford, CT.

102. GTS—Prescott File #6, December 26, 1862.

103. Mason, op. cit., p. 247 ff.

104. GTS—Library.

105. MDA—Chrystal to Whittingham, November 2, 1863.

106. MDA—Bound Pamphlets, vol. 18, no. 30.

107. Robert Cheney Smith, SSJE, The Cowley Fathers in America, the Early Years, published by the S.S.J.E., no date, p. 2-3.

108. Cameron, Kenneth W., The Catholic Revival in Episcopal Connecticut, Hartford: Transcendental Books, 1965.

109. MDA—Prescott to Whittingham, March 6, 1866.

110. GTS—Prescott File #3.

111. Cameron, op. cit., p. 191.

112. Grafton, Charles C., The Works of Bishop Grafton, ed. B. Talbot Rogers, vol. 7, "Letters and Addresses," New York: Longmans, Green & Co., 1914. p. 28 ff.

113. Ibid., pp. 31 ff.

114. Ibid., pp. 42 ff.

115. Ibid., p. 57.

116. Ibid., p. 64.

117. Ibid., p. 69.

118. Connecticut Diocesan Journal, 1867.

119. CDA—C.P. Prescott, The Cross of Christ, A Lenten Sermon preached in Christ Church, West Haven, bound pamphlets, vol. 126.

120. Grafton, op. cit., p. 79.

121. MDA—Prescott to Whittingham, March 8, 1868.

122. MDA—Dr. G. C. Shattuck to Whittingham, November 12, 1869.

123. Dictionary of American Biography, vol. 17, pp. 32-33.

124. GTS—Prescott File #8, February 6, 1870.

125. A Brief History & Description of St. Clement's Church, Philadelphia, Published by the Parish, no date.

126. MDA—Shattuck to Whittingham, 1871.

127. MDA—Shattuck to Whittingham, February 21, 1872.

128. MDA—Shattuck to Whittingham, February 22, 1872.

129. Robert Cheney Smith, SSJE, The Cowley Fathers in America, the Early Years, published by the Society of St. John the Evangelist, no date.

130. Community Archives, Community of St. John the Baptist, Mendham, New Jersey.

131. E.A. White & J.A. Dykman, Annotated Constitution and Canons . . . of the Episcopal Church, New York: Seabury Press, 1981 edition, vol. 1, pp. 442 ff.

132. Pennsylvania Diocesan Archives, Prescott to Bishop John Wiliams.

133. Pennsylvania Diocesan Archives, Prescott to Bishop Stevens, January 21, 1876.

134. Pennsylvania Diocesan Archives, Bishop Stevens to Prescott, April 21, 1876.

135. Pennsylvania Diocesan Archives, Bishop Stevens to Prescott, July 26, 1876.

136. GTS—Prescott File #11, includes three letters pertaining to Prescott's inhibition by the Bishop of Montreal.

137. SSJE Archives, Prescott File.

138. GTS—Prescott File #12, October 19, 1876.

139. GTS—Prescott File #14, includes copies of Bishop Stevens' letters of October 18, 30 to Prescott and Prescott's reply to Stevens of November 14.

140. GTS—Prescott File #13, November 8, 1876.

141. GTS—Prescott File #14, November 14, 1876.

142. GTS—Bound Pamphlets, The Prescott Case, includes "Report of the Committee of Inquiry Appointed by the Convention of the Diocese of Pennsylvania in the Matter of St. Clement's Church," Philadelphia, 1879, p. 31.

143. Ibid., p. 29 ff.

144. Ibid., p. 32.

145. Ibid., p. 33.

146. Ibid., p. 34.

147. Ibid., p. 34.

148. Ibid., p. 35.

149. Ibid., p. 36 ff.

150. Ibid., p. 37 ff.

151. Ibid., p. 38.

152. SSJE—Prescott File.

153. GTS—Prescott File #17.

154. GTS—Prescott File #19.

155. GTS—Prescott File #21, 22, 23, 24, 25 & 26.

156. GTS—Prescott File #27.

157. SSJE—Archives, Prescott File.

158. GTS—Prescott File #28.

159. SSJE—Prescott File.

160. Anonymous Pamphlet, "What It Meant & How It Was Done," A Review of Proceedings in the late Diocesan Convention of Pennsylvania held May 6-9, 1879, published by several members of the Convention, Philadelphia, 1879. The full text of the 1878 Resolution is printed on pp. 4 & 5.

161. GTS—Prescott File #29 contains copies of two letters.

162. GTS—Prescott File #30.

163. GTS—Prescott File #29.

164. Prescott File #31.

165. GTS—Prescott File #32.

166. GTS—Prescott File #33.

167. GTS—Prescott File #36.

168. GTS—Bound Pamphlets, The Prescott Case, op. cit., pp. 39 ff.

169. MDA—2 letters from Prescott to Whittingham and one from Whittingham to Prescott.

170. GTS—Bound pamphlets, The Prescott Case.

171. Ibid.

172. Ibid.

173. Ibid.

174. Ibid.

175. Ibid.

176. Ibid.

177. Ibid.

178. GTS—Prescott File #38.

179. GTS—Bound Pamphlets, The Prescott Case.

180. GTS—Prescott File #39.

181. SSJE—Prescott File.

182. GTS—Bound Pamphlets, The Prescott Case.

183. GTS—Prescott File #40.

184. GTS—Prescott File #41.

185. GTS—Bound Pamphlets, The Prescott Case.

186. GTS—Prescott File #42.

187. GTS—Bound Pamphlets, The Prescott Case.

188. SSJE—Prescott File.

189. George E. DeMille, The Catholic Movement in the Episcopal Church, Philadelphia: Church Historical Society, 1941, p. 125.

190. William W. Manross, A History of the American Episcopal Church, New York: Morehouse, 1935, p. 306.

191. GTS—Bound Pamphlets, The Prescott Case.

192. GTS—ibid.

193. GTS—Prescott File #45.

194. GTS—Prescott File #47, 46 and #48 are partial drafts of this letter.

195. GTS—Prescott File #49 and #50.

196. GTS—Prescott File Box 2, #25.

197. Adam D. McCoy, Holy Cross, A Century of Anglican Monasticism, Wilton, Ct.: Morehouse-Barlow, 1987, pp. 13 ff.

198. Robert W. Adamson, Father Huntington's Formative Years (1854-1892): Monasticism and Social Christianity, Columbia University: Dissertation, 1971, pp. 62-63.

199. GTS—Prescott File #51.

200. GTS—Prescott File #52.

201. Robert Cheney Smith, The Cowley Fathers in America, The Early Years, published by the Society of St. John the Evangelist, no date, p. 23.

202. Vestry Minutes, St. Clement's Church, Philadelphia, PA.

203. Robert Cheney Smith, op. cit., pp. 19-20.

204. Vestry Minutes, St. Clement's Church, Philadelphia, PA.

205. Ibid.

206. Ibid.

207. Robert Cheney Smith, op. cit., p. 26.

208. GTS—Prescott File #55. This six page item includes copies of several letters to Prescott and one from him.

209. Ibid.

210. Ibid.

211. Vestry Minutes, St. Clement's Church, Philadelphia, PA.

212. Robert Cheney Smith, op. cit., p. 25.

213. GTS—Prescott File #56.

214. GTS—Prescott File #59.

215. SSJE—Prescott File.

216. Robert Cheney Smith, op. cit., p. 71.

217. SSJE—Prescott File.

218. Ibid.

219. Ibid.

220. Ibid.

221. Grafton, C.C., Works, vol. 7, p. 86.

222. Glenn Johnson, "Grafton: The Bishop," in The Beacon, Michaelmas, 1988, p. 39.

223. SSJE—Prescott File.

224. GTS—Prescott File #60.

225. Grafton, Works, vol. 7, p. 87.

226. McCoy, Holy Cross, p. 39.

227. GTS—Prescott File #61.

228. S.S.J.E.—Prescott File, February 17, 1885, February 20, 1885.

229. Ibid.

230. GTS—Prescott File #63

231. SSJE- Prescott file, April 12, 1885.

232. Grafton—<u>Works</u>, vol. 7, p. 89 ff.

233. SSJE—Prescott File, October 16, 1885.

234. Grafton, <u>Works</u>, vol. 7, p. 112.

235. SSJE—Prescott File, May 27, 1885.

236. Grafton, <u>Works</u>, vol. 7, p. 113.

237. Ibid., pp. 114-115.

238. SSJE—Prescott File, May 22, 1888.

239. William K. Tinkham, "Grafton: Priest & Pastor," in <u>The Beacon</u>, Michaelmas, 1988, p. 33.

240. SSJE—Prescott File, May 22, 1888.

241. Ibid., May 26, June 1, June 4 and June 12, 1888.

242. GTS—Prescott File #75.

243. SSJE—Prescott File, June 7, 1888.

244. Tinkham, op. cit., p. 34.

245. SSJE—Prescott File, November 14, 1888.

246. Ibid., January 24, 1889.

247. Ibid., March 14, 1889.

248. GTS—Prescott File #79.

249. Tinkham, op. cit., p. 34.

250. SSJE, Prescott file Easter Monday, April 22, 1889

251. SSJE—Prescott File, October 26, 1889.

252. New York Diocesan <u>Journal</u>, 1889.

253. GTS—Prescott File Box 2, #68.

254. GTS—Prescott File Box 2, #9 and 10.

255. GTS—Prescott File Box #85.

256. MASS.

257. GTS—Prescott File #88.

258. GTS—Prescott File #90.

259. McCoy, <u>Holy Cross</u>, p. 66.

260. Connecticut Diocesan <u>Journal</u>, 1904, Prescott Obituary.

261. Jill M. Snyder, <u>St. Luke's Parish, 1844-1944</u>, published by the Parish, New Haven, CT., 1996, p. 17.

262. GTS—Bishops' Letters.

263. GTS—Prescott File #42.

264. Grafton, <u>Works</u>, vol. 7, p. 117

265. GTS—Bishop's Letters.

266. Jill M. Snyder, op. cit., p. 18.

267. <u>New Haven City Directories</u>, 1893 through 1900.

268. SSJE—Prescott File.

269. GTS—Prescott File #94.

270. Grafton, <u>Works</u>, vol. 7, p. 118.

271. GTS—Prescott File, Box 2, #21.

272. GTS—Prescott File, Box 1, #99.

273. GTS—Prescott File Box 1, #98.

274. GTS—Prescott File, Box 2, #18.

275. Christ Church, New Haven Parish Register, p. 272.

276. Cameron, <u>Catholic Revival in Episcopal Connecticut</u>, p. 264.

277. CDA—Aged and Infirm Clergy Fund records.

278. GTS—Prescott File, Box 2, #57, #58, #60, and #61.

279. McCoy—<u>Holy Cross</u>, p. 47.

280. GTS Library.

281. GTS Library, <u>The Nazareth Chronicle</u>.

282. SS JE.—Prescott File.

283. Connecticut Diocesan <u>Journal</u>, 1904.

284. <u>The Living Church</u>, December 5, 1903